Carolyn Humphries has been a food writer and ed[i]
years. She started her career as a chef, but quickl[y]
preferred to create food for people to cook at h[ome]
trained as a journalist, she became a food writ[er]
magazine. She has since written for numerous m[agazines]
author of more than 60 books and has been a[s]
writer and editor on many more projects. She is
of the Guild of Food Writers and the In[stitute]
Promotion and Education.

Also available from Robinson

Everyday Lebanese Cooking

Feast of Vegetables, Pulses, Herbs and Spices

y Family Recipes for Your Combination
Microwave

Everyday Cooking for One

Everyday Thai Cooking

Everyday Curries

ealthy Slow Cooker Cookbook

ditional Country Preserving

Bread from Your Bread Machine

How To Make Perfect Panini

o Make Your Own Cordials and Syrups

Southern Italian Family Cooking

Afternoon Tea

Pâtisserie

THE HIGH-SPEED BLENDER COOKBOOK

Carolyn Humphries

A How To Book

ROBINSON

ROBINSON

First published in Great Britain in 2015 by Robinson

A CIP catalogue record for this book is available from the British Library.

ISBN: 978-1-47213-648-0 (paperback)

Typeset by Basement Press, Glaisdale
Printed and bound in Great Britain by Clays Ltd, Elcograf S.p.A.

Papers used by Robinson are from well-managed forests
and other responsible sources

MIX
Paper from
responsible sources
FSC® C104740

Robinson
is an imprint of
Little, Brown Book Group
Carmelite House
50 Victoria Embankment
London EC4Y 0DZ

An Hachette UK Company
www.hachette.co.uk

www.littlebrown.co.uk

How To Books are published by Robinson, an imprint of Little, Brown Book Group. We welcome proposals from authors who have first-hand experience of their subjects. Please set out the aims of your book, its target market and its suggested contents in an email to howto@littlebrown.co.uk

CONTENTS

CONTENTS

INTRODUCTION

I've always had a large goblet blender as part of my food mixer, plus a hand blender for puréeing soups and other things directly in the saucepan, so I was a bit sceptical about the need to have this new, all-singing, all-dancing blender. But the name is misleading. This isn't just a blender – it's a whole new kitchen appliance.

Having tried a juicer and being appalled at the waste of all the goodness of the whole fruit and vegetables left behind in the machine (which was a real nuisance to clean), I was intrigued to discover that this machine would blend up even the toughest stalks and grains to a smooth, delicious drink or soup that would include every bit of the fibre and phytonutrients*. What a great way to get kids – or anyone else who's reluctant about eating a variety of fruit and vegetables – to eat way more of them and to get every iota of goodness they contain! There are smaller blenders that just do this, but this book is designed for use with a large, multi-purpose machine that can do so much more.

When I first bought my high-speed blender, I was surprised to see that the cookbook that came with it didn't show me how to do half the things I'd been led to believe it would do. This was disappointing as it needed to justify its place on my precious work surface – and the hefty price! So I started to put it through its paces and create great recipes to get the absolute maximum out of my machine. I had many highs and a few lows before coming up with this selection, but I'm convinced that it shows you just how versatile and efficient this machine can be and covers all the opportunities it offers. And I hope it will help and inspire you to go on and create even more exciting recipes using the principles I've employed.

The high-speed blender is so much more than a blender or food processor, although it can blend the velvetiest smoothies, the smoothest pre-cooked soups and silkiest drinks. It can whiz up from scratch *and cook* divine, smooth soups and sauces; make the lightest batters I've ever created; create creamy nut butters and other pâtés and spreads; whiz up frittatas ready to pop into the pan; whisk *and freeze* ice creams and sorbets; grind flour, coffee beans and spices; make doughs and cake mixes; and finely chop or purée just about anything you need to prepare. And, most importantly, it does it all in the blink of an eye. It is an odd beast, though. Some things I thought would be brilliant just didn't work at all – such as finely chopped vegetables, zabaglione and shortbread – while others totally wowed me – like bread dough, scones and Yorkshire puddings.

The ice cream it makes is extraordinary. It takes literally a minute from start to finish. I don't promise it's the best you have ever tasted (especially if you usually use an ice cream maker) because you use loads of ice cubes to freeze it and the ice, unavoidably, dilutes the flavour a little. But if you want a soft, whipped ice to cool down the kids or for a speedy dessert, then it's brilliant. If you are aiming for firmer results, you just freeze the ice cream once it has blended for a few hours, then store it in the freezer for another day. Those made with frozen fruit are the best, in my opinion (see page 140); as you don't need extra ice.

To get the maximum benefit from your machine, keep it out on the work surface. Don't stick it in a cupboard so you have to take it out every time you want to make a milkshake. Have it to hand and use it to its full potential. It could become a daily kitchen friend to save you time, effort and money, in the long term, as it costs very little to run.

I bought an Optimum 9400 Domestic and Commercial High-speed Blender but there are several others on the market. If you use a different machine, operating instructions and blending times may vary slightly. Check the power output of your machine. If it's lower than mine (mine whizzes up at 4800rpm and is 1500w), you may need to extend your timings slightly – but literally only by seconds. Simply check the food during and at the end of processing. If necessary, you can always tag on a few extra seconds. Likewise, if your general instructions for various types of recipes differ from mine, follow your machine's operating instructions.

---

*Phytonutrients in fruit and vegetables give us powerful antioxidants to boost the immune system and combat free radicals. These are unstable molecules that are made by oxygen in our bodies all the time, but production is accelerated through unhealthy lifestyle. They attack the DNA, then attach themselves to healthy cells, damaging them, which may cause heart disease and some cancers.

CHAPTER 1
ABOUT YOUR BLENDER – HOW IT WORKS AND HOW TO LOOK AFTER IT

You want to make the most of your machine, so it makes sense to find out how it works and how to keep it working well.

The main way a high-speed blender differs from an ordinary one is that it has an incredibly powerful motor for such a small machine. This, coupled with precision blades, allows it to pulverise food very quickly, however tough or hard it is.

The high-powered motor, if run for several minutes, creates enough friction to heat a purée, thus giving you hot soup or sauce in minutes. This high speed also means it can crush and purée frozen fruit and veg, or blend them with ice cubes to make an ice cream or sorbet consistency so fast that it doesn't have time to melt. (You have to watch you don't over-process, of course, or all your good work will be undone as it will begin to heat up and so melt again.)

My machine has one virtually unbreakable blender goblet to do all tasks. Some makes have a separate dry container for grinding flour or kneading dough. Personally I like to have the single utensil as it's easier to store and means you never make a mistake using the wrong container!

To make the most of your machine, just take a look at these simple, common-sense guidelines.

ORDER OF INGREDIENTS

- Whatever you are doing, always put the liquids in first.
- Then add softer foods.
- Add hard items and ice last.

TO MAKE AND HEAT SOUPS AND SAUCES

You can use hot or cool liquids but if you use hot stock for soup, for instance, it will heat up more quickly.

- Put the liquids into the jug but never fill above the 2-litre mark.
- Add any other ingredients, following the order of ingredients above.
- Secure the lid (check your operating instructions for how to do this as they all differ slightly).
- Select Variable Speed 1. Switch on the machine. Gradually increase to Variable Speed 10 or the maximum speed for your machine. Process at this high speed until your mixture is really hot and thickened, if necessary. The outside of the goblet should feel piping hot and plenty of steam will escape.

See also Top Tips in Chapter 4 (see pages 41–43).

WET AND DRY CHOPPING

To chop, you can just put the foods you want chopped into the blender goblet, although remember that the blender does process very quickly so you can't really chop coarsely. Secure the lid. Select Variable Speed 1. Switch on the machine and gradually increase to a medium speed, usually between 3 and 5, then chop the food to the desired size, using the tamper to press the ingredients onto the blades, if necessary. BEWARE, as this happens extremely quickly and it is easy to over-process the food at the bottom while food on the top is still whole. So if you want to just chop a few ingredients and then remove them from the blender, rather than combine a whole mixture, do it in small quantities – it only takes a few seconds, after all!

Alternatively, for soft, delicate foods, you can put them in the goblet, select Variable Speed 1, 2 or 3 and pulse the machine a few times by switching it on and off quickly. Some machines have a pulse button but they are not all as convenient as you would think. On mine, you have to switch on the machine before using the pulse, so the blades are still whizzing round all the time and it over-processes, negating the quick burst of power you want.

For chopping hard fruits and vegetables, you can 'wet chop' them. Simply put chunks of the ingredients in the blender goblet with enough water to cover so they float off the blades, then pulse the machine a couple of times to chop (once or twice for roughly, three or more times for finely). Then you can drain off the water. I find this method is particularly good for onions or potatoes as it removes the strong taste of onion and the starch from the potatoes. For other fruit and vegetables, use the liquid in the dish when possible, as some of the nutrients, such as water-soluble vitamins, and flavour will have leached into the water.

The machine will make a loud noise and you may get some hot smell from the motor, particularly when processing mixtures that require the tamper. Don't worry, this is normal. However, I do stress, it's always better to stop the machine and let it rest briefly if the mixture is difficult to process, otherwise you could overheat and damage the motor (the more you use the machine, you will get used to knowing what is normal and what is not).

USING THE TAMPER

The tamper is used through the hole in the blender goblet lid to press ingredients on to the blades. This keeps the food circulating and prevents air pockets forming, which would impair the blending process. It's particularly useful when there is no added liquid present, such as for nut butters, puréed or chopped fruit and veg, chopped/minced meat or ice creams with lots of ice cubes to grind up.

- Always use the tamper through the properly secured lid.
- The goblet should not be more than two-thirds full when using the tamper.
- Don't use for more than 30 seconds without a rest or the machine may overheat.
- You may sometimes need to guide the tamper towards the edges rather than just pushing straight down to make sure no air bubbles get trapped and prevent the food from moving freely.
- You may also need to stop the machine and scrape down the sides with a spatula (particularly if making a small quantity).

REMOVING FOOD FROM THE GOBLET

One of the few downsides to these blenders is the laborious business of removing some mixtures, as access round the blades is very limited.

- For thicker pastes and even thick soups, you do need a good, flexible spatula to scrape out the food from under the blades. A small, long-handled spoon, too, is often useful to get the last of it!
- For doughs and other heavy mixtures, when processing is complete, pulse the machine once or twice to lift the mixture

off the blades. You should then be able to remove it easily. (If necessary, for stickier mixtures, when you've got most of it out, try replacing the goblet on the motor, secure the lid and pulse once or twice again – it often releases the last bits from the blades.)

• Use a wet spatula to remove any bits of sticky dough or paste stuck to the sides and blades.

AUTOMATIC OVERLOAD PROTECTION

Most machines have an overload protection switch (mine is on the base). If the machine overheats, which can happen if you are blending thick contents for too long, it will cut out. Simply allow the machine to cool down for a while. It may be fine when you try it again – if not, reset the switch.

CLEANING AND MAINTENANCE

Do not put any part of the blender in the dishwasher – always follow the manufacturer's instructions below.

CLEANING THE GOBLET
1 Half-fill the goblet with warm water and add a couple drops of washing-up liquid.
2 Secure the lid.
3 Select Variable Speed 1. Switch on the machine and gradually increase to Variable Speed 10 (or maximum for your machine).
4 Run the machine for 10–60 seconds, depending on what had been in the machine.
5 Switch off the machine, then empty it out, rinse, then turn the jug upside down to dry. Or, if you need to use it again

immediately, dry inside and out with a soft cloth, taking care when putting your hand in because the blades are sharp!

6   Before you use the blender again, check the base of the jug where the cog is. If it is still wet, dry thoroughly with a soft cloth.

CLEANING THE LID AND TAMPER

1   Wash in the sink in warm, soapy water, then rinse.
2   Dry with a soft cloth.

TO DEEP-CLEAN WHEN NECESSARY

If you use your blender frequently, my manufacturer recommends giving it a thorough clean once a month.

1   Half-fill the goblet with white vinegar and top up with cool water.
2   Leave to stand for 12–24 hours.
3   Pour away contents, then follow the normal cleaning instructions above, running the machine for 10–20 seconds.

CLEANING THE MOTOR BASE

1   Unplug the machine from the power source.
2   Use a soft, damp cloth or sponge to wipe over the surface, taking special care between and around the knobs and switches. Use soapy water if there are dried food particles on the surface.
3   Polish with a soft, dry cloth to finish.

CLEANING THE CUSHION PAD

1   First remove the blender goblet, then remove the cushion pad from the base.

2   Wipe over the pad using a damp cloth rung out in warm soapy water or, if necessary, submerge in the sink. Drain and rinse.
3   Wipe dry with a soft cloth.
4   Before putting back on the base, check the underside of the base to ensure it is free from any liquid or food residue and, if necessary, clean with a damp cloth rung out in soapy water then dry with a soft cloth.

TARNISHED BLADES

Should the blades discolour over time, simply cover the blades with white vinegar and leave to soak for 24 hours, then rinse thoroughly.

CHAPTER 2
A HEALTHY DIET

It is vitally important to good health to eat a balanced diet, selecting the right proportions of food from each of the main food groups. You will be familiar with the usual division into carbohydrates, proteins and so on, but I think it is more useful to group them according to what you actually eat, so you should have foods from all the following groups on a daily basis. The 'eatwell' plate shows you the proportions of each food group that you should be aiming for.

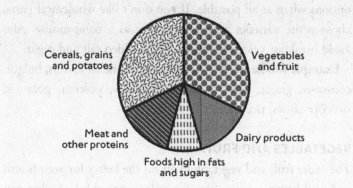

Cereals, grains and potatoes

Vegetables and fruit

Meat and other proteins

Dairy products

Foods high in fats and sugars

Now that you are using your high-speed blender you will be getting more natural fibre from your fruit and vegetables in particular. This will aid your digestion and can help prevent serious gut disorders. If you are not used to a high-fibre diet and now start to eat many more fruits, vegetables and grains, you may experience some bloating and wind and, even, a bit of a 'runny tummy'. This is normal and is simply a result of your body adjusting to the new diet. It should only be temporary. However, if you do experience any problems, just cut back a bit on the new blender soups and smoothies and introduce these high-fibre meals gradually. But do persevere and you will reap the benefits in the long term.

CEREALS, GRAINS AND POTATOES

These are starchy carbohydrates – the fuel to give you the energy to do everything from sleeping and thinking to running a marathon – and they should make up about one-third of what you eat every day. They will also fill you up, keep you warm and provide natural soluble and insoluble fibre. Go for wholegrain options when at all possible. If you don't like wholemeal pasta, chose white varieties with added fibre as a compromise. Also avoid breakfast cereals that are high in added salt and sugar.

Example foods: Every type of bread, breakfast cereals, bulgur, couscous, grains, oats, pasta, pearl barley, polenta, potatoes, sweet potatoes, rice, yams.

VEGETABLES AND FRUIT

The more fruit and vegetables you eat the better for your health and well-being – again, aim for at least one-third of what you eat. They provide essential vitamins, minerals, phytonutrients (see page 3) and fibre and will help prevent diabetes, heart disease and cancer.

You should aim to eat at least five portions a day, preferably seven. A portion is half an avocado or mango, a good wedge of melon; 1 banana, orange, apple, pear, peach or nectarine; 2–3 smaller fruit, such as plums or clementines, depending on size; a large handful of berries; a glass of pure juice or an average serving of vegetables (about 80g or 3 heaped tablespoons).

Note that as fruit juice doesn't contain any fibre, it only counts as one of your five-a-day, however much you drink. Although, made in your high-speed blender, using the whole fruit or vegetable, each glassful counts towards your total.

Example foods: Every type of fruit and vegetable you can lay your hands on – fresh, frozen, dried, canned (in natural juice or water), plus pure fruit and vegetable juices.

MEAT AND OTHER PROTEINS

Proteins are vital for the growth and repair of all body tissue. Around one-sixth of your daily intake should come from protein foods.

Example foods: You'll find protein in red meat such as lamb, pork, beef and venison; poultry; fish; eggs (it's the white that contains the protein); and vegetable sources such as dried peas, beans and lentils, nuts, seeds and soya products, such as tofu.

DAIRY PRODUCTS

Milk, cheese and yoghurt provide calcium for healthy teeth and bones as well as protein, vitamins and minerals. If you don't get enough, you risk osteoporosis (brittle bones) in later life as well as rotten teeth. However, they are high in fat so many people prefer to choose low-fat options, where appropriate. Edam cheese is naturally lower in fat than other hard cheeses and is very versatile. This is an important group that should be about one-sixth of your daily intake.

If you can't tolerate dairy products, you can get enough calcium from other sources. Do not cut out dairy products from your diet unless advised to by a doctor.

Example foods: Dairy products are all types of cheeses from fromage frais and ricotta to camembert, cheddar, parmesan and all different blue chesses, yoghurt and milk. Other sources of calcium include oats; soya, sunflower, nut or rice milks enriched with calcium; dried fruit; eggs; and dark green vegetables, such as spinach and broccoli. Canned fish with bones is also a good source if you eat the bones too!

FATS

Fats, eaten in moderation, are important to keep the brain functioning properly, for cell formation, to keep our skin supple, for energy and to keep us warm. They also play a vital role in the absorption of fat-soluble vitamins (A, D, E and K). If you eat too much of any fat it will contribute towards obesity so should be avoided. However, some fats are better for you than others, so aim for the 'good' fats as part of your balanced diet.

Saturated fat can clog up the arteries and lead to high, 'bad' LDL blood-cholesterol levels, which, in turn, can lead to heart disease, strokes and some cancers. Always choose lean meat, don't eat the skin of poultry and don't eat crackling (well, OK, but only a little bit!). Some people prefer to choose reduced-fat milk, cheese and yoghurt, particularly if weight-watching or if there is a history of heart disease and strokes in the family.

However, for those who like butter, there is nothing wrong with having a scraping on bread or using a knob in cooking. The flavour is second to none. Just don't slap it on bread with a trowel!

Example foods: Meat and poultry; dairy products, such as milk, butter, cheese and yoghurt.

The second group is polyunsaturated fats. They contain omega-3 and omega-6 essential fatty acids to help aid a healthy heart, blood, eyes, brain and immune system.

Example foods: Egg yolks, fish, nut, seed and vegetable oils.

The third type is monounsaturated fats. They're known to help reduce 'bad' LDL cholesterol in the bloodstream and help raise 'good' HDL cholesterol. That's why so many people choose to follow a Mediterranean-style diet, where olive oil is the fat of choice and they eat a lot of fish, fruit and vegetables.

Example foods: Avocados, olives, nuts, seeds and their oils.

SUGARS

There's a lot of confusion about sugar. All sugars are simple carbohydrates but not all sugars are bad for you. Some foods contain sugars that appear naturally as part of their make-up. Such foods are fine to eat as they are a good source of 'instant' energy and also provide the body with loads of other nutrients as well. The only caveat is that if you consume a lot of sweet fruits, particularly dried fruits, or drink a lot of pure fruit juice, they can still damage the enamel on teeth, so brush regularly with a fluoride toothpaste.

Example foods: Fruit, vegetables, milk, nuts, seeds and grains.

The sugars to avoid are the *added* refined sugars, whether brown or white or in syrup form – as they just pile on 'empty' calories, which can lead to obesity and tooth decay. Sugar, surprisingly, appears on the ingredients list of many foods from soups to sauces, bread to ready-meals, so it is worth checking the ingredients label for added sugar. This is more useful than reading the nutritional label which doesn't differentiate between added sugar and that found naturally in the ingredients.

Trendy fructose and agave syrup are just as bad as granulated, caster, muscovado or demerara. Keep added refined sugar of any sort to a minimum. Have sweet, sugary foods as occasional treats rather than filling up on them on a daily basis. When sweetening foods, I prefer to use unrefined honey as it contains antioxidants and some vitamins and minerals and is thought to have probiotic properties (so helps to keep your gut healthy), but it should be used still only in moderation.

SALT

Salt occurs naturally in everything we eat and enhances the flavour of many foods. I do use added salt in moderation in cooking for that reason. However, use it judiciously and keep it to a minimum (use other flavourings to enliven your food, such as herbs, spices, vinegars, and citrus juice and zest) as it is recommended that we don't have more than 6g a day (that's about 1 tsp!).

Example foods: Salt, processed and cured meats, such as ham, sausages and bacon, salted nuts, pickles, salted and smoked fish, stock cubes, ready-meals

NOTES ON THE RECIPES

- If you can, invest in a set of accurate digital scales. They will measure even tiny quantities in metric or imperial, liquids and solids, so you can pop the blender goblet on the scales and simply measure in everything you need. Spoon ingredients in slowly a bit at a time, though, because it's easy to add more, not so easy to remove (but, as the liquids go in first, the extra solids can be carefully spooned out if you absolutely have to!).

- The ingredients are listed in the order in which they are used in the recipe.

- All spoon measures are level unless otherwise stated: 1 tsp = 5ml; 1 tbsp = 15ml.

- Eggs are medium unless otherwise stated.

- Individual vegetables or fruits are average-sized unless otherwise stated, for example, 1 potato = 1 average-sized (or medium) potato.

- A handful is the amount you can hold comfortably in the palm of your hand.

- Always wash fresh fruit and vegetables before use. When using the high-speed blender you only need to peel, core or deseed if the recipe says you should. If blending into a soup or smoothie, it will completely process the core and seeds too. I only take off brown calyxes or hard stalks in pale-coloured mixtures so tiny flecks don't show in the finished dish.

- Use fresh herbs unless dried are specified.

- The use of strong flavourings such as chilli or garlic are a matter of personal preference. Always use your own judgement and reduce or increase the quantity according to your taste.

- Some dishes just have to be sweetened. I have used honey in preference to sugar in many recipes (except when only sugar will do in some baked recipes) but you can substitute caster sugar for honey in any recipe, if you prefer. Always add a small amount, taste and add more if necessary. The ripeness of the fruit, for instance, will make a difference to how much sweetener is needed.

- All can and packet sizes are approximate as they vary from brand to brand. For example, if I call for a 400g can of tomatoes and yours is a 410g can – that's fine.

- All blending times are approximate. It will often depend on the size of the ingredients added. Smaller pieces will blend faster than larger ones and ripe fruit will purée more quickly than hard ones.

- Cooking times are approximate and should be used as a guide only. Always check food is piping hot and cooked through before serving.

- Always preheat the oven and cook on the shelf just above the centre unless using a fan oven where preheating and the positioning are not so crucial.

- When making recipes that you are going to heat in the blender, such as a soup or sauce, use boiling or very hot liquids, when possible, and other ingredients at room temperature rather than straight from the fridge to speed up the heating process.

- Use screw-top bottles or other sealable containers to store your foods. To sterilise jars or bottles, put them through a dishwasher cycle or wash them thoroughly in hot water, then rinse and dry out in a warm oven (at 160ºC) for 30 minutes. Alternatively, providing they don't have any metal clasps, half-fill with water, place in the microwave and microwave on HIGH for a few minutes or until the water is boiling rapidly then drain and place upside down on kitchen paper to dry.

CHAPTER 3
HEALTH-GIVING DRINKS, SPECIALITY MILKS AND SMOOTHIES

Your high-speed blender can do a much better job than a juicer for drinks because you can process the whole fruit or vegetables to give you all the nutrients in a smooth and delicious form. It also makes wonderful speciality milks from nuts or grains, which can be used in place of cows' milk in any of the recipes. Try some of my rich packed-with-goodness smoothies, too, and they'll get you well on the way to your five a day! They're thick and velvety with the addition of banana, avocado, buttermilk, yoghurt or nuts to enrich and give the luxurious texture we all adore.

NUT MILK

Experiment with different nuts for delicious health-giving alternatives to cows' milk. For maximum goodness, don't strain.

Makes about 750ml

90g whole, raw almonds, cashews or peanuts
450ml cold water
1 tbsp apple juice (optional)

1   Put the nuts in a bowl and cover with cold water. Leave to soak for several hours, or preferably overnight.
2   Strain the nuts, then tip them into the blender goblet and add the measured water and the apple juice, if using. Secure the lid.
3   Select Variable Speed 1. Switch on the machine and gradually increase to Variable Speed 10 (or maximum for your machine). Blend for 45 seconds or until smooth.
4   Pour into a sterilised bottle or container with a sealable lid. Alternatively, for an extra-smooth texture, strain through a muslin (or new disposable kitchen cloth) lining a sieve.
5   Store in the fridge for up to 5 days. Shake well before use.

OAT MILK

You can sweeten this with a tablespoon of apple juice if you prefer a slightly less bland flavour.

Makes about 1 litre

115g porridge oats
800ml cold water
a pinch of salt

1   Put the oats and water in a bowl. Cover with a lid or a clean tea towel and leave to soak for several hours or overnight.
2   Tip the contents of the bowl into the blender goblet and add the salt. Secure the lid.
3   Select Variable Speed 1. Switch on the machine and gradually increase to Variable Speed 10 (or maximum for your machine). Process for 40 seconds until smooth.
4   For best nutrition, pour unstrained into a sterilised bottle or container with a sealable lid. Alternatively, for an extra-smooth texture, strain through a muslin (or new disposable kitchen cloth) lining a sieve.
5   Store in the fridge for up to 5 days. Shake well before use.

KALE, EDAMAME AND GINGER VITALITY SHOT

Look out for naturally fermented soy sauce to give you healthy probiotic properties, which are good for the gut. I use a reduced-salt variety but you can use any dark soy sauce, though bear in mind, a higher-salt one will give a saltier tang.

Serves 1

120ml pure orange juice
a large handful of kale (about 25g)
a handful of frozen, shelled edamame (soya) beans (about 30g)
1 tsp reduced-salt soy sauce
1cm piece of fresh root ginger, peeled
1 tsp clear honey
6 ice cubes

1 Put all the ingredients in the blender goblet in the order listed. Secure the lid.
2 Select Variable Speed 1. Switch on the machine and gradually increase to Variable Speed 10 (or maximum for your machine). Blend for 20–30 seconds until smooth.
3 Pour into a glass and serve immediately.

CUCUMBER AND YOGHURT LASSI WITH CARDAMOM AND MINT

A cooling and refreshing drink when the temperature soars, this is also ideal to sip with or after eating a hot curry to douse the fire!

Serves 1

100ml semi-skimmed milk
100ml plain yoghurt
5cm piece of cucumber, halved lengthways, plus 1 slice,
    to garnish
2 green cardamom pods
1 sprig of mint
a pinch of salt
6 ice cubes

1   Put all the ingredients except the cucumber garnish in the blender goblet in the order listed. Secure the lid.
2   Select Variable Speed 1. Switch on the machine and gradually increase to Variable Speed 10 (or maximum for your machine). Blend for 30 seconds until smooth.
3   Pour into a glass and serve with a slice of cucumber resting on the rim.

STRAWBERRY AND ELDERFLOWER FIZZ

Strawberries and elderflowers make a wonderful flavour combination but this also works really well with blueberries or some stewed, lightly sweetened rhubarb.

Serves 1

100g strawberries, hulled
½ tsp lemon juice
2 tbsp elderflower cordial
4 ice cubes
chilled sparkling mineral water

1 Put the strawberries, lemon juice, elderflower cordial and ice cubes in the blender goblet. Secure the lid.
2 Select Variable Speed 1. Switch on the machine and gradually increase to Variable Speed 10 (or maximum for your machine). Blend for 20–30 seconds until smooth.
3 Pour into a glass, top up with sparkling mineral water and stir well. Serve straight away.

BERRY REFRESHING

I like this drink quite sharp as it is so thirst-quenching on a sunny day, but if you have a sweet tooth you can add a little honey or, if you must, some caster sugar. You can substitute blackberries for strawberries for a change, too.

Serves 1

a handful of strawberries, hulled
a handful of raspberries
a handful of blueberries
2 thin slices of fresh unwaxed lime
200ml cloudy pure apple juice
4 ice cubes
clear honey (optional)

1 Put all the berries and 1 slice of the lime into the blender goblet, then add the apple juice and ice cubes. Secure the lid.
2 Select Variable Speed 1. Switch on the machine and gradually increase to Variable Speed 10 (or maximum for your machine). Process for 20 seconds until smooth.
3 Taste and add 1–2 teaspoons of honey if not sweet enough for your palate. Secure the lid and blend briefly again.
4 Pour into a glass and hang a slice of lime over the rim of the glass.

ICED CHAI LATTE

If you pour slowly, you can leave the tea leaf sediment at the bottom of the goblet but you can use a tea strainer if you prefer.

Serves 1

200ml ice-cold milk
2 tsp clear honey
1 chai tea bag, leaves only
3 ice cubes
freshly grated nutmeg, to garnish

1 Put the ingredients into the blender in the order listed. Secure the lid.
2 Select Variable speed 1. Switch on the machine and blend for 30 seconds, then leave to stand for 30 seconds.
3 Slowly pour into a glass mug, leaving the leaf sediment behind. Serve straight away.

WATERCRESS, GREEN TEA AND ORANGE PICK-ME-UP

Packed with vitamin C and antioxidants, this is a drink to set you up the morning after the night before – or just any time you need a boost. If you aren't keen on the peppery taste of watercress, try it with spinach or lettuce instead.

Serves 1

150ml pure orange juice
a handful of watercress (about 15g)
1 orange, peeled and broken in half
1 green tea bag, leaves only
12 green grapes
2 tsp clear honey
4 ice cubes

1　Put the ingredients in the blender goblet in the order listed. Secure the lid.
2　Select Variable Speed 1. Switch on the machine and gradually increase to Variable Speed 10 (or maximum for your machine). Blend for 40 seconds until smooth.
3　Pour into a glass and serve straight away.

THICK NECTARINE AND ALMOND MILKSHAKE

You could use fresh apricots or a peach in place of the nectarine. Alternatively, if fresh aren't available, try a small can of fruit in natural juice – if you include the juice, too, it'll make enough for two glasses. You could pop a spoonful or two of dried milk powder in, too, if you are using canned fruit, to enrich it further.

Serves 1

150ml ice-cold milk
1 nectarine, halved and stoned
1 small handful of whole almonds (about 30g)
1 tsp clear honey
2 ice cubes

1 Put the ingredients in the blender goblet in the order listed. Secure the lid.
2 Select Variable Speed 1. Switch on the machine and gradually increase to Variable Speed 10 (or maximum for your machine). Blend for 20–30 seconds until smooth.
3 Pour into a glass and serve straight away.

BROCCOLI, PEANUT BUTTER AND JALAPEÑO ZING

This is for those of you who prefer a savoury hit of nutrients and it gives you three of your five a day. If you prefer a fruit and vegetable blend, omit the chilli and salt and use 100ml orange juice and 4 tbsp plain yoghurt instead of buttermilk.

Serves 1

150ml buttermilk
2 tbsp cold water
1 large handful of fresh shelled or frozen peas (about 80g)
1 large or 2 smaller tomatoes, halved
½ jalapeño (or other fat green chilli), seeded (optional)
2 good-sized broccoli florets (about 80g)
2 tsp peanut butter
a pinch of salt
freshly ground black pepper
3 ice cubes

1 Put all the ingredients in the blender goblet in the order listed. Secure the lid.
2 Select Variable Speed 1. Switch on the machine and gradually increase to Variable Speed 10 (or maximum for your machine), using the tamper to press the ingredients onto the blades. Blend for 20–30 seconds until smooth and thick.
3 Pour into a tall glass and serve immediately.

BREAKFAST SMOOTHIE

Packed with vitamins, minerals and energy, this smoothie is the perfect way to start the day when you haven't got time to sit down and enjoy a 'proper' breakfast. If you don't want to drink it before you leave the house, pour it into a bottle or vacuum flask and take it with you to have when you reach your destination (or en route if you can).

Serves 1

200ml ice-cold milk
1 small banana, peeled
1 apple or pear, quartered and cored
1 small handful of raisins
2 tbsp porridge oats or instant oat cereal
1 tbsp whole raw hazelnuts or almonds

1   Put all the ingredients in the blender goblet in the order listed. Secure the lid.
2   Select Variable Speed 1. Switch on the machine and gradually increase to Variable Speed 10 (or maximum for your machine). Blend for 30 seconds until smooth.
3   Pour into a large glass and serve.

CARROT, CLEMENTINE AND SOYA SMOOTHIE

Using the peel of one of the clementines means you get all the lovely zesty oil to enhance the flavour. Using peel from all three is a bit too strong (but it's not much effort to peel two of them!). The tofu adds a mild creaminess and, of course, a good dose of protein and phytonutrients (see page 3).

Serves 1

150ml pure orange juice
1 large carrot, scraped or peeled and cut into chunks
75g silken tofu
3 clementines, 2 peeled, 1 whole and washed

1 Put all the ingredients in the blender goblet in the order listed. Secure the lid.
2 Select Variable Speed 1. Switch on the machine and gradually increase to Variable Speed 10 (or maximum for your machine). Blend for 40 seconds until smooth.
3 Pour into a glass and serve straight away.

AVOCADO, KIWI, PEAR AND PUMPKIN SEED SMOOTHIE

This is a green smoothie at its best. Not only is it packed with health-giving nutrients, it tastes divine! Some people find kiwi fruit sort of tickle the back of the throat – if so, use a couple of greengages, halved and stoned, when in season, or a small green apple instead. It makes a great substitute quick meal any time of day. If you like your smoothies very cold, throw in a couple of ice cubes before blending.

Serves 1-2

1 small (or ½ larger) avocado, halved, stoned and peeled
1 kiwi fruit, peeled
1 pear, stalk removed and quartered (no need to core or peel)
1 tbsp pumpkin seeds
8–10 mint leaves
150ml ice-cold milk

1 Put the ingredients in the blender goblet in the order listed. Secure the lid.
2 Select Variable Speed 1. Switch on the machine and gradually increase to Variable Speed 10 (or maximum for your machine). Blend for 20 seconds until smooth.
3 Pour into 1 or 2 glasses and serve straight away.

PHYTONUTRIENT SPECIAL SMOOTHIE

This is simple and simply delicious. Packed with phytonutrients that are thought to help prevent heart disease and some cancers, it's a refreshing snack-cum-drink any time of day.

Serves 1

200ml natural, unsweetened coconut water
1 banana, peeled
80g juicy pomegranate seeds (apils)

1 Put the ingredients in the blender goblet in the order stated. Secure the lid.
2 Select Variable Speed 1. Switch on the machine and gradually increase to Variable Speed 10 (or maximum for your machine). Blend for 30–40 seconds until smooth.
3 Pour into a glass and drink straight away.

PINEAPPLE, PASSION FRUIT AND COCONUT SMOOTHIE

Because you need half a small can of pineapple per person, I have made this smoothie serve two people. If you prefer, you can make half the quantity and store the remaining pineapple in an airtight container in the fridge to whip up another smoothie in a day or so. You can use a low-fat or no-fat yoghurt if you prefer.

Serves 2

2 passion fruit
180ml Greek-style plain yoghurt
160ml can coconut cream
227g can pineapple chunks or slices in natural juice
8 stoned dates

1 Halve the passion fruit and scoop the seeds and pulp into the blender goblet. Add the remaining ingredients in the order listed. Secure the lid.
2 Select Variable Speed 1. Switch on the machine and gradually increase to Variable Speed 10 (or maximum for your machine). Blend for 40 seconds until smooth.
3 Pour into 2 glasses and serve immediately.

BLUEBERRY PIE

The rich purple flavonoids in blueberries and blackberries – called anthocyanins – are thought to be particularly good for keeping the heart and eyes healthy, so it's worth enjoying one of these vibrant smoothies regularly. If you pick wild blackberries in late summer or early autumn you may need to add a little more honey or more dried fruit as the berries will be sharper.

Serves 1

150ml Greek-style plain yoghurt
6 tbsp cold milk
a large handful of blueberries (about 80g)
a large handful of blackberries (about 80g)
1 tsp lime juice
2 tbsp porridge oats
1 tbsp raisins or dried blueberries
2 ice cubes

1 Put the ingredients in the blender goblet in the order listed. Secure the lid.
2 Select Variable Speed 1. Switch on the machine and slowly increase to Variable Speed 10 (or maximum for your machine). Blend for 40 seconds until smooth.
3 Pour into a glass and serve straight away.

SPICED BANANA AND MANGO SMOOTHIE

This is just so delicious – the fragrant mango goes so well with creamy banana, while the dried apricots add natural sweetness and extra nutrients.

Serves 1–2

200ml cold milk
1 banana, peeled
½ mango, flesh only
4 soft, ready-to-eat dried apricots
¼ tsp ground cinnamon
a little freshly grated nutmeg
2 ice cubes

1 Put the ingredients in the blender goblet in the order listed. Secure the lid.
2 Select Variable Speed 1. Switch on the machine and gradually increase to Variable Speed 10 (or maximum for your machine). Blend for 30 seconds until smooth. Taste and add more nutmeg if necessary.
3 Pour into a glass and serve straight away.

PEACH MELBA SMOOTHIE

This is really a pudding in a glass – but just as good at 8am as 8pm! For a luxury (if less healthy) version, add a scoop of vanilla ice cream instead of the ice cubes.

Serves 1

150ml buttermilk
¼ tsp natural vanilla extract
1 small banana, peeled
a large handful of raspberries (about 80g)
1 peach or nectarine, halved and stoned
1 tsp clear honey
4 ice cubes

1 Put the ingredients in the blender goblet in the order listed. Secure the lid.
2 Select Variable Speed 1. Switch on the machine and gradually increase to Variable Speed 10 (or maximum for your machine). Blend for 30-40 seconds until most of the raspberry seeds have been processed.
3 Pour into a glass and serve straight away.

CHAPTER 4
HOT AND CHILLED SUSTAINING SOUPS

Dish up soups in record time with your high-speed blender. They are yet another great way to get in masses of veggies to top up your five-a-day. All these soups have minimal preparation – as that's what this blender excels at – being able to blend up from raw – but you can use cooked veggies and just whiz and heat, as in my Bubble and Squeak Soup (see page 46) or of course, use it in the normal way – cook your soup in a pan, then pop it in your high-speed blender to purée it in double-quick time. It's particularly useful if you've cooked stringy vegetables, like beans or celery, in a soup, which would normally need sieving after puréeing. This machine is so powerful it simply processes them completely.

TOP TIPS FOR MAKING HOT SOUPS FROM RAW INGREDIENTS

- Never use raw white, yellow or red onion as it's too strong. Leek or spring onion will give better results. I also use dried onion for a quick onion hit. If you do want to use a fresh onion, first sauté it in a knob of butter or a splash of olive oil for 2 minutes until softened slightly and translucent. You can do the same for leeks if you prefer a milder flavour in your soup.

- Never use raw potato. If you want to put potato in your soup, use leftover cooked potato, drained canned potatoes, or wash a largish one, prick all over with a fork and microwave on High for about 4 minutes or until it is soft, then chop it and add to the blender goblet. Other starchy vegetables, such as parsnip or celeriac, that you could also eat raw, are fine to use uncooked.

- Good thickeners are instant oat cereal, canned dried beans or lentils, canned potatoes or leftover cooked ones, or bread. You can also blend in cooked rice or pasta.

- Use boiling stock or other hot liquid, when possible, to kick-start the heating process.

- Use other foods at room temperature rather than straight from the fridge, when possible, as, again, it helps reduce the heating time.

- Don't fill the blender goblet more than two-thirds full when you are using hot liquid.

- Remember that all the flavours will be in their natural taste, so greens for example can be quite strong, as it will be like eating them raw. For some vegetables with milder flavours, like carrots, you may need to use quite a lot to get a rich taste – which is great to help you hit your five a day.

- Be judicious with spices and herbs. If you are making a curried soup, a paste will give a better flavour than a powder as it won't leave a residual powdery taste in your finished soup. Dried herbs are very strong. Use them sparingly as, again, they don't have time to 'cook into' the soup, which would make them more mellow in flavour. I use fresh ones most of the time, but, occasionally, you want the specific flavour dried can bring.

- I like my soup piping hot. Sometimes I find that the recommended maximum time for blending of 6 minutes is not quite enough. I switch off the machine and leave it for a minute or two, then blend for a further minute or until the soup is absolutely piping hot.

- If you are making soup to reheat later, there is no need to blend for the 6 minutes. Just blend the ingredients until really smooth – usually 20–30 seconds – then tip into an airtight container and store in the fridge. It's then quicker to reheat the soup in a saucepan or in the microwave than in the blender.

THAI RED CURRY, VEGETABLE AND CASHEW NUT SOUP

This soup is just packed with flavour and goodness. You could make a green soup in the same way, but use a handful of thawed frozen or fresh peas or mangetout in place of the pimiento caps, substitute green pepper for red, and use turnip instead of carrot – and, of course, Thai green curry paste (see page 165 or use shop-bought) instead of the red paste.

Serves 4

4 heaped tbsp raw whole cashew nuts
4 tbsp boiling water
2 pimiento caps, from a jar
2 tomatoes, skinned and halved
1 tbsp chopped coriander
450ml boiling vegetable stock
400ml can coconut milk
2 tsp Thai fish sauce
4 spring onions, trimmed and roughly cut up
1 stalk of lemongrass, roughly chopped
1 large carrot, peeled and cut in rough chunks
1 parsnip, peeled and cut in rough chunks
1 red pepper, halved, stalk removed and deseeded
6 pieces of sun-dried tomato in oil, drained
2 tbsp Thai Red Curry Paste (see page 166 or use shop-bought)
1cm piece of fresh root ginger, peeled
salt and freshly ground black pepper

1   Soak the cashew nuts in the boiling water for 15 minutes.
2   Put the pimiento caps and skinned tomatoes in the blender goblet. Secure the lid.
3   Select Variable Speed 1. Switch on the machine and pulse 3 or 4 times to chop. Scoop into a small bowl, mix in the coriander and set aside.
4   Tip the nuts with any soaking water into the blender goblet and add the stock. Add the remaining ingredients in the order listed. Secure the lid.
5   Select Variable Speed 1. Switch on the machine and gradually increase to Variable Speed 10 (or maximum for your machine). Blend for 5–6 minutes until the blender goblet feels piping hot and masses of steam escapes when you take off the lid.
6   Pour into warm bowls and top with the chopped pimiento, tomato and coriander garnish before serving.

BUBBLE AND SQUEAK SOUP WITH SOFT POACHED EGGS AND CRISPY BACON

This is the perfect way to use up leftover potatoes and cabbage – the quantities don't matter much but it should be about half and half. I like to fry them off in a pan before adding to get that 'bubble and squeak' flavour. You can omit this stage but the taste is definitely not as good. You could use cauliflower or even green beans instead of cabbage if that's what you have. If you fancy making it and don't have any ready-cooked veggies, simmer equal quantities of potatoes and shredded cabbage in the stock until tender, then tip into the blender and continue as below.

Serves 4

For the soup
200g cooked potatoes
200g cooked cabbage
a knob of butter
750ml boiling chicken stock
2 tbsp dried onions
1 tbsp thyme leaves, including any soft stalks
3 tbsp dried milk powder
¼ tsp smoked paprika
1 tbsp Worcestershire sauce, plus extra to serve
salt and freshly ground black pepper

To serve
4 streaky bacon rashers
4 fresh eggs
1 tbsp white wine vinegar or a large pinch of salt

1 Chop up the potatoes if in large pieces. Fry with the cabbage in the butter for about 3 minutes until fragrant and lightly golden.

2 Put the stock in the blender goblet and add the potato and cabbage mixture and the remaining ingredients. Secure the lid.

3 Dry-fry the bacon in a frying pan until crisp. Then drain on kitchen paper and snip into small pieces. Set aside.

4 Bring a shallow pan of water to the boil with the vinegar or salt added, then reduce to a simmer.

5 While the water is coming to the boil, select Variable Speed 1 on the blender. Switch on the machine and gradually increase to Variable Speed 10 (or maximum for your machine). Blend for 5–6 minutes until the goblet feels piping hot and masses of steam escapes when you take off the lid.

6 Meanwhile, break the eggs one at a time into a cup and slide into the water. Poach for 2–3 minutes, or until cooked to your liking.

7 Taste the soup and re-season if necessary. Ladle into warm shallow bowls. Lift the eggs out of the pan with a slotted spoon and float an egg in each bowl. Sprinkle with the crispy bacon and add a few drops of Worcestershire sauce.

CHESTNUT AND MUSHROOM VELOUTÉ

This soup is rich, thick and velvety. If you prefer a slightly thinner soup, simply increase the stock to 900ml.

Serves 4

2 tbsp dried porcini mushrooms
2 tbsp dried onions
4 tbsp boiling water
200g chestnut mushrooms
a knob of butter
4 tsp brandy
750ml boiling chicken or vegetable stock
240g can cooked, peeled chestnuts
1 tsp dried oregano
salt and freshly ground black pepper
120ml single cream

1 Soak the dried mushrooms and onions in the boiling water for at least 5 minutes but preferably 15 minutes.
2 Meanwhile, thinly slice 2 of the mushrooms. Heat a little butter in a small frying pan and sauté the mushrooms until soft and lightly golden. Pour off any juices into the blender goblet and set the cooked mushrooms aside.
3 Put the soaked mushrooms and onions and the stock in the blender goblet. Add the brandy and the remaining raw mushrooms, the chestnuts, oregano and some salt and pepper. Secure the lid.

4 Select variable Speed 1. Switch on the machine and gradually increase to Variable 10 (or maximum for your machine). Blend for 5–6 minutes until the goblet feels piping hot.

5 Remove the bung from the lid (take care as steam will escape) and pour in the cream. Secure the lid again and blend for a further 1 minute to heat. Taste and re-season.

6 Ladle into warm soup bowls and garnish with a few sliced cooked mushrooms.

WHITE BEAN, CARROT AND CUMIN SOUP

Carrot and cumin and are always good together and here the white beans add substance. You need a lot of carrots when using from raw to give a good, rich, sweet flavour but as carrots are so cheap it really isn't a problem, and they're so good for you.

Serves 4

750ml boiling vegetable or chicken stock
400g can white kidney or butter beans, drained
1 tbsp olive oil, plus extra to garnish
a handful of coriander leaves, plus a little chopped to garnish
2 tbsp dried onion
900g carrots, peeled or trimmed and scrubbed and cut into
    chunks
2 tsp ground cumin
2 tbsp tahini paste
1 tsp clear honey
salt and freshly ground black pepper
thick plain yoghurt, to garnish

1 Put all the ingredients in the blender goblet in the order listed. Secure the lid.
2 Select Variable Speed 1. Switch on the machine and gradually increase to Variable Speed 10 (or maximum for your machine). Blend for 5 minutes, or until the goblet feels piping hot and masses of steam escapes when you take off the lid. Taste and re-season, if necessary.
3 Ladle into warm soup bowls and add a dollop of yoghurt, a drizzle of olive oil and a sprinkling of chopped coriander to each bowl.

LEEK, CHEESE AND CELERIAC SOUP

This has a vibrant colour and intense flavour. If you like a milder onion taste, slice the leek and sauté in the knob of butter for 3 minutes, stirring until slightly softened but not browned, before adding to the blender goblet with the remaining ingredients.

Serves 4

750ml hot vegetable or chicken stock
4 tbsp dried milk powder
4 tbsp instant oat cereal
1 large leek (about 300g), washed well, trimmed and cut into lengths
½ celeriac (about 400g), peeled and cut into chunks
a knob of butter
2 sprigs of thyme
5 sprigs of parsley, plus extra, chopped, to garnish
100g strong Cheddar cheese, cubed
salt and freshly ground black pepper

1   Put all the ingredients in the blender goblet in the order listed. Secure the lid.
2   Select Variable Speed 1. Switch on the machine and gradually increase to Variable Speed 10 (or maximum for your machine). Blend for 5–6 minutes until the goblet feels piping hot and masses of steam escapes when you take off the lid.
3   Taste and re-season, if necessary. Ladle into warm bowls and top each with a tiny sprig of parsley.

TOMATO SOUP – PLAIN AND SIMPLE

This is best made in the summer when local ripe tomatoes are available, as they are by far the most flavoursome (use 900g). However, here I've used a can of tomatoes, too, to top up the taste, which means you can enjoy the soup all year round. Using dried onion ensures you don't get any 'raw' onion flavour in the finished soup as it's only heated up rather than cooked for any length of time.

Serves 4

600ml hot chicken or vegetable stock
5 tbsp instant oat cereal
4 tbsp dried milk powder
400g can plum tomatoes
2 tbsp dried onions
500g fresh tomatoes
2 tbsp tomato purée
2 tbsp clear honey
1 tsp dried mixed herbs
2 tsp sweet paprika
salt and freshly ground black pepper
6 tbsp double cream

1   Put all the ingredients except 2 tbsp of the cream in the blender goblet in the order listed. Secure the lid.
2   Select Variable Speed 1. Switch on the machine and gradually increase to Variable Speed 10 (or maximum for your machine). Blend for 6 minutes until the goblet feels piping hot and the mixture is thick and smooth.
3   Taste and re-season, if necessary. Pour into soup bowls and garnish with a swirl of the remaining cream.

HERBY GREENS SOUP

This is perfect for nutrition in a bowl! You simply put everything in the blender and whiz. No fuss, no effort and masses of goodness!

Serves 4

750ml hot vegetable or chicken stock
4 tbsp instant oat cereal
200g kale, roughly chopped
1 courgette, trimmed and cut into chunks
2 spring onions, trimmed and cut into chunks
1 turnip, peeled and quartered
a handful of parsley
a large sprig of rosemary, picked leaves only
1 tsp clear honey
salt and freshly ground black pepper
4 tbsp crème fraîche

To serve
grated Parmesan cheese

1   Put all the ingredients except the crème fraîche and Parmesan into the blender goblet in the order listed. Secure the lid.
2   Select Variable Speed 1. Switch on the machine and gradually increase to Variable Speed 10 (or maximum for your machine). Blend for 5 minutes, or until the goblet feels piping hot.
3   Open the lid and add the crème fraîche. Secure the lid again and blend for a further 30 seconds–1 minute.
4   Taste and re-season, if necessary. Serve in bowls, topped with plenty of grated Parmesan cheese.

SPINACH AND AVOCADO SOUP WITH PRAWNS

Vibrant green and refreshing, this soup is ideal for a summer party, with its mild and creamy flavour. For vegetarians, use vegetable stock instead of chicken and omit the prawns but garnish instead with a little crumbled feta cheese. Low-fat or no-fat Greek-style yoghurt is fine, if you prefer.

Serves 6

200ml Greek-style plain yoghurt
450ml cold chicken stock
300ml cold milk
2 spring onions, trimmed
250g spinach
2 avocados, halved, stoned and peeled
a handful of dill
¼ cucumber
1 tbsp lemon juice, or to taste
salt and freshly ground black pepper
6 ice cubes
120g cooked, peeled prawns, thawed if frozen

1 Put all the ingredients except the prawns in the blender goblet in the order listed. Secure the lid.
2 Select Variable Speed 1. Switch on the machine and gradually increase to Variable Speed 10 (or maximum for your machine). Blend for 20 seconds until smooth.
3 Taste the soup and re-season or add more lemon juice, if necessary. Pour into shallow bowls and garnish each one with a small mound of cooked, peeled prawns.

CHILLED APPLE AND CREAM CHEESE SOUP WITH CHOPPED WALNUTS

This is a really nutritious soup that can be served for a starter or dessert or, even, for breakfast!

Serves 4

30g walnut pieces
200ml cloudy pure apple juice
250g cream cheese (or use low-fat white soft cheese)
2 tbsp clear honey
¼ tsp ground cloves
4 green eating apples, quartered with stalk, pips and calyx removed
4 ice cubes
1 tbsp walnut oil

1 Put the walnuts in the blender goblet. Secure the lid.
2 Select Variable Speed 3. Switch on the machine and pulse a few times by switching the machine on and off to chop the nuts fairly finely. Tip them out and set aside for garnish. Leave any residual finely ground nuts in the base of the goblet.
3 Put all the remaining ingredients except the oil in the blender goblet in the order listed. Secure the lid.
4 Select Variable Speed 1. Switch on the machine and gradually increase to Variable Speed 10 (or maximum for your machine). Blend for 40 seconds or until smooth.
5 Pour into shallow soup bowls and drizzle with a little walnut oil. Top with a generous sprinkling of chopped walnuts and serve.

ASPARAGUS, PEA AND MINT SOUP

This is the perfect soup for a hot summer's day – it's fresh, it's vibrant and it takes just minutes to make. You can use fresh shelled peas if you can get young ones, soon after picking, but using frozen guarantees the perfect, sweet result and helps to chill the soup at the same time. It can be served hot, too, in which case, use thawed frozen peas and boiling stock. Blend for 5–6 minutes or until the blender goblet feels very hot and when you remove the lid, plenty of steam escapes.

Serves 4–6

1 bunch of asparagus (about 250g), cut in short lengths
225g frozen petit pois, plus 1 tbsp for garnish
300ml milk
450ml cold chicken or vegetable stock
75ml crème fraîche, plus 1 tbsp for garnish
2 tsp lemon juice
1 spring onion, trimmed and roughly cut up
a handful of mint leaves (about 7g), plus small sprigs for garnish
salt and freshly ground black pepper

1   Select 4–6 of the asparagus spear heads (depending on how many you are serving) for garnish. Blanch them in a little boiling water with the tablespoonful of frozen peas for 2 minutes, then drain, rinse with cold water and drain again. Set aside.

2   Put the milk, stock and crème fraîche in the blender goblet. Add the rest of the asparagus and peas, then the remaining ingredients in the order listed. Secure the lid.

3   Select Variable Speed 1. Switch on the machine and gradually increase to Variable Speed 10 (or maximum for your machine). Blend for 30 seconds, or until really smooth. Taste and re-season, if necessary.

4   Pour into wide shallow soup bowls and garnish each one with a small dollop of crème fraîche, an asparagus spear head, a few petit pois and a tiny sprig of mint. Serve immediately.

CHAPTER 5
DIPS, PÂTÉ, SPREADS AND FONDUES

Most people love foods you can dip into with gorgeous crusty bread, toast, crackers or fresh vegetable or fruit crudités. They also enjoy foods that can be spread on scrummy receptacles, like pâtés or nut butters on toast, or homemade jam or fruit spread on freshly baked scones. Here you'll find an array of the most delicious and nutritious ones – all with new twists – that can be whizzed up in minutes in your high-speed blender ready to tickle your taste buds all hours of the day.

CHICKEN LIVER PARFAIT

If you only have a normal blender or food processor, to get the velvety smooth texture of a parfait you would have to do the laborious work of pushing the blended mixture through a fine sieve. With your high-speed blender, however, you simply cook the ingredients, then whiz them up ultra quickly, pack in little pots and chill to firm. If you are going to keep the parfait for a few days, coat the tops in a thin layer of melted butter to seal and prevent air getting in.

Serves 4–6

75g butter
400g chicken livers
1 garlic clove, peeled
2 tbsp brandy
6 tbsp double cream
salt and freshly ground black pepper
chopped parsley, to garnish

To serve
**wholegrain toast, pickled gherkins and sweet fruit chutney
  or cranberry sauce**

1 Melt the butter in a frying pan. Add the chicken livers and garlic and sauté for 4–5 minutes until browned and cooked but still soft. Add the brandy and ignite. Shake the pan until the flames subside.

2 Tip into the blender goblet and add the cream and some salt and pepper. Secure the lid.

3 Select Variable Speed 1. Switch on the machine and gradually increase to Variable Speed 10 (or maximum for your machine). Blend for 20 seconds until smooth.

4 Spoon into 4–6 small ramekin dishes and level the surface. Cover with clingfilm and chill until firm. Garnish with chopped parsley and serve with some wholegrain toast and pickled gherkins, sweet fruit chutney or cranberry sauce.

SMOKED PAPRIKA HUMMUS

Everyone loves hummus as a healthy and nutritious snack or dip so I wanted to come up with a slightly different flavour combination. Adding the spicy, smoky chorizo gives it a whole new dimension. However, if you are vegetarian, simply omit it. You'll still get a mild smokiness from the smoked paprika.

Serves 4-6

90ml olive oil, plus extra for drizzling
1 tbsp lemon juice
1 tbsp tahini paste
1 garlic clove, peeled
400g can chickpeas, drained
½ tsp smoked paprika
salt and freshly ground black pepper
60g chorizo, finely diced (optional)

To serve
pitta bread strips and/or crudités

1 Put all the ingredients except the chorizo in the blender goblet in the order listed. Secure the lid.

2 Select Variable Speed 1. Switch on the machine and gradually increase to Variable Speed 10 (or maximum for your machine). Blend for 30 seconds, pressing the ingredients against the blades with the tamper. Taste and re-season if necessary, adding more lemon juice, if liked.

3 If using the chorizo, add now and pulse the machine (by switching on and off quickly) once or twice to mix in. Scoop into a small bowl, drizzle with a little olive oil and serve with pitta bread strips and/or crudités.

GUACAMOLE WITH GREEN PEPPER AND FRESH GREEN CHILLI

The simplest Mexican guacamole is made with just plenty of crushed avocado and some fresh lime juice but there are loads of variations of this popular dip. This is my take on it and it packs a bit of a punch. If you prefer a milder chilli flavour, scrape out the seeds before use.

Serves 4–6

1 small green pepper, quartered and seeded
1 green jalapeño chilli, stalk removed
1 small shallot, peeled and halved
1 firm tomato
a small handful of coriander
2 tbsp extra-virgin olive oil
1 large avocado, halved, stoned and peeled
juice of 1 lime
a pinch of salt
freshly ground black pepper
a few drops of Worcestershire sauce

To serve
crudités and tortilla chips

1 First put the pepper, chilli, shallot, tomato and coriander in the blender goblet. Secure the lid.

2 Select Variable Speed 1. Turn on the machine and pulse twice to roughly chop (don't overdo it as it'll get mixed in and chopped a tiny bit more later). Tip out the chopped ingredients and reserve.

3 Put the remaining ingredients in the blender goblet (no need to wash it). Secure the lid.

4 Select Variable Speed 1. Switch on the machine and gradually increase to Variable Speed 6. Blend for 10 seconds until smooth.

5 Add the chopped ingredients, secure the lid again and pulse the machine 2 or 3 times to blend them in. Taste and re-season, adding more salt, pepper, lime juice or Worcestershire sauce as required.

6 Spoon into a small bowl (or individual pots) and serve with crudités and tortilla chips.

DILL AND ANCHOVY PESTO

This is gorgeous stirred through pasta, thinned with olive oil and a squeeze of lemon as a sauce for fish or a salad dressing (especially with crisp croûtons added), or stirred into mayonnaise and mixed with prawns or smoked salmon as a sandwich filling.

Makes about 250g

90ml extra-virgin olive oil, plus extra for storing
1 bunch of dill (about 50g)
50g can anchovies in oil
1 tbsp lemon juice
2 tbsp freshly grated Parmesan
1 garlic clove, peeled
75g pine nuts
salt and freshly ground black pepper

1 Put all the ingredients in the blender goblet in the order listed but add pepper not salt at this stage. Secure the lid.
2 Select Variable Speed 1. Switch on the machine and gradually increase to Variable Speed 10 (or maximum for your machine), pressing the ingredients onto the blades with the tamper. Blend for about 30 seconds until smooth.
3 Taste and add salt if necessary (it should be quite strong but you can always season more when you use it). Spoon into a sterilised screw-topped jar or other sealable container and pour a thin layer of oil over the surface to keep the air out. Store in the fridge. It will keep for several weeks as long as you keep the sides of the jar clean and the contents covered with a layer of oil.

TAHINI AND CUCUMBER DIP

I know I've used tahini paste quite a few times in this book but it adds so much flavour, texture and goodness to so many dishes – I just love it! Here the toasted sesame flavour blends beautifully with cooling cucumber and smooth mayonnaise.

Serves 4

6 tbsp mayonnaise (see page 96 or use good-quality bought)
2 tbsp tahini paste
2 tbsp crème fraîche
salt and freshly ground black pepper
grated zest of ½ lemon
1 tsp lemon juice
1 tbsp toasted sesame oil, plus extra for drizzling
5cm piece of cucumber, quartered

To serve
thin flatbreads, olives and radishes

1   Put the ingredients except the cucumber in the blender goblet. Secure the lid.
2   Select Variable Speed 1. Switch on the machine and gradually increase to Variable Speed 4 to blend the tahini into the mixture, then switch off.
3   Add the cucumber. Secure the lid again. Select Variable Speed 3. Switch on the machine and pulse a few times until the cucumber is chopped and mixed into the sauce ingredients.
4   Scoop out into a small bowl. Taste and re-season if necessary, then cover with clingfilm and chill in the fridge until ready to serve with thin flatbreads, olives and radishes.

CASHEW NUT BUTTER WITH SALT FLAKES

You can make other nut butters in exactly the same way. They make simple, delicious and nutritious spreads to top bread, crackers, slices of cucumber or to spoon into chicory or celery 'boats'. They can be made into sauces – such as satay, the popular spicy peanut sauce served with grilled meat – stirred through pasta or added to stews or casseroles to enrich them. Omit the salt for a plain butter. You don't have to add any flavourings but you might like to experiment – try almonds with a pinch of ground mixed spice, or peanut butter, perhaps enhanced with a little Szechuan pepper. Your blender makes nut butter so quickly but the one drawback is it's a bit of a fiddle to get out of the goblet – keep wetting the spatula and persevere (the result is well worth it, and at least the goblet is very easy to clean (see page 9)!

Makes about 300g

4–6 tbsp sunflower oil
250g raw cashew nuts
½ tsp sea salt flakes

1 Put 4 tbsp of the oil and the nuts in the blender goblet. Secure the lid.

2 Select Variable Speed 1. Switch on the machine and gradually increase to Variable Speed 10 (or maximum for your machine), using the tamper to press the ingredients on the blades.

3 Blend for about 30 seconds then stop and scrape down the sides. Secure the lid again, switch on the machine and blend for a further 30 seconds, again using the tamper as necessary until as smooth as you like your nut butter, adding a little more oil if necessary.

4 Gently stir the sea salt flakes through the paste (don't try to do this with the machine running). Spoon the nut butter into a clean screw-topped jar, using a wet spatula to scoop out the butter stuck around the blades and up the sides.

5 Store in the fridge. It will keep for several weeks.

PEAR AND APPLE SPREAD

This wonderful no-added-sugar 'butter' spread is delicious on bread or toast or spooned over ice cream. The dates give it an almost caramelised sugar taste – the perfect combination with apples and pears. There's no need to core the fruit.

Makes about 300g

75g butter, melted
1 red eating apple, quartered
1 pear, quartered
100g stoned dates
2 tsp lemon juice

1 Put all the ingredients in the blender goblet in the order listed. Secure the lid.
2 Select Variable Speed 1. Switch on the machine and gradually increase to Variable Speed 6, using the tamper to push the ingredients onto the blades. Blend for 1 minute until really smooth.
3 Spoon into a clean screw-topped jar (I use two small ones) and chill to firm slightly.
4 Store in the fridge and use within a week or two. If you want it to keep longer, cover the spread in a layer of melted butter that will harden and seal against the air. Carefully lift off before using. Alternatively, the mixture can be frozen.

FRESH STRAWBERRY AND APRICOT SPREAD

You can use raspberries, blueberries or blackberries in place of strawberries for other delicious 'jam' alternatives. Apart from using it as jam you can also dollop it in plain yoghurt or fold into whipped cream or custard for a fruit mousse or fool.

Makes about 300g

55g ready-to-eat dried apricots
4 tbsp boiling water
250g strawberries, hulled
1 tsp lemon juice
1 tbsp clear honey
2 tbsp chia seeds

1   Put the apricots and boiling water in a bowl and leave to soak until cold. The apricots will absorb the liquid.
2   Put the apricots in the blender goblet with half the strawberries, then lemon juice and honey and secure the lid. Select Variable Speed 1, switch on the machine and gradually increase to Variable Speed 10 (or maximum for your machine). Blend for 15 seconds until smooth.
3   Add the remaining strawberries and the chia seeds and secure the lid. Select Variable Speed 1. Switch on the machine and gradually increase to Variable Speed 4. Turn the dial back to Variable Speed 1 and switch off the machine (there should still be some small pieces of strawberries).
4   Leave in the container for 10 minutes, pulsing the machine briefly every few minutes so the chia seeds thicken the mixture but don't clump together.
5   Spoon into a sterilised jar and chill in the fridge for several hours before using, then store in the fridge for up to about a week.

THREE-CHEESE FONDUE

Making a fondue normally takes lots of gentle stirring over a hot stove, but using your high-speed blender takes all the hard work out of it! You can vary the cheeses as you wish – or even use all Swiss cheese if you prefer. I first made this using cornflour in the normal way. It worked absolutely fine but there was a slight powdery aftertaste as the mixture doesn't actually boil to cook out the starch. I therefore now make it with instant oats when serving it in ramekins. If you prefer to use cornflour, use just 1 tbsp instead of the oat cereal (and that is fine if you are going to leave it bubbling in a fondue pot for a little while before eating).

Serves 4–6

150ml milk
1½ tbsp kirsch or white wine
2 tbsp instant oat cereal
1 small garlic clove, peeled
75g Emmental or other Swiss cheese, cubed
75g Cheddar cheese, cubed
75g Red Leicester cheese, cubed
a good pinch of cayenne
salt and freshly ground black pepper

To serve
chunks of French bread and crudités

1 Put all the ingredients in the blender goblet in the order listed. Secure the lid.

2 Select Variable Speed 1. Switch on the machine and gradually increase to Variable Speed 10 (or maximum for your machine). Blend for 6 minutes, or until the goblet feels piping hot and the mixture is thick and glossy. If necessary, let the machine rest a minute, then blend for a further minute to reach the desired consistency.

3 Pour into a fondue pot over its heat, or individual ramekins and serve straight away, with chunks of French bread and crudités to dip into it.

CHOCOLATE AND MARSHMALLOWS FONDUE

Rich, wicked and delicious, this fondue will touch the spots that other desserts just can't reach! It's lovely to serve each guest a double espresso coffee to sip as they eat – the perfect contrast of bitter versus sweet.

Serves 4-6

150ml boiling water
40g dried milk powder
60g white marshmallows, snipped in pieces with wet scissors
150g dark chocolate, broken in pieces
a little milk, if necessary

To serve
whole strawberries, slices of pear or apple (tossed in lemon juice to prevent browning), orange segments, ratafias or plain finger biscuits or sponge fingers

1 Put all the ingredients except the milk in the blender goblet in the order listed. Secure the lid.
2 Select Variable Speed 1. Switch on the machine and gradually increase to Variable Speed 10 (or maximum for your machine). Blend for 3 minutes until the mixture is thick and the goblet feels hot, stopping and scraping down the sides once or twice during blending. Thin with a little milk if too thick and blend again.
3 Spoon into a fondue pot and keep warm, or into individual ramekins and serve straight away, with the pieces of fruit, and ratafias, finger biscuits or sponge fingers.

CHAPTER 6

WHIZZED-UP BATTERS AND OMELETTE MIXES

When you make batters traditionally, you need to hold the bowl and whisk vigorously until they're smooth and blended. Your high-speed blender will take all the hard work and effort out of it. For frittatas and tortillas, too, no more laborious chopping or mixing. Just whiz and cook! I've just made a frittata and tortilla here but you could just whiz up eggs with cheese or spinach or other flavourings and cook as an omelette in a little melted butter.

BUCKWHEAT GALETTES

Galettes originated in Brittany, France. They are the perfect receptacles for simple savoury fillings. Try them just with grated Emmental or Gruyère chese; with a slice of ham and a slice of cheese; cheese, ham and a fried egg; spinach and ricotta cheese with plenty of freshly grated nutmeg; slices of Camembert with some grilled bacon; prawns, sliced cherry tomatoes and mayonnaise ... you name it!

Makes 8-10

300ml milk
1 large egg
115g buckwheat flour
a pinch of salt
60g butter, melted
a little sunflower or groundnut oil, for frying

1   Put the milk, egg, flour and salt in the blender goblet. Secure the lid.
2   Select Variable Speed 1. Switch the machine on and gradually increase to Variable Speed 10 (or maximum for your machine). Blend for 20 seconds.
3   Turn down to Variable Speed 1 again. Remove the plug in the lid and pour in the melted butter. Leave the machine running for 2–3 seconds to blend.

FRENCH STYLE SWEET CREPES

4   Heat a little oil in a 23cm non-stick frying pan until really
    hot. Pour off any excess. Pour in enough batter to swirl
    round the pan and thinly coat the base. Fry until the
    underside is golden brown, the surface is dry and it is quite
    crisp around the edges and lacy in texture (don't undercook
    or the galette, which is very thin, will break up on turning).
    Flip it over and briefly cook the other side. If it is not quite
    crisp and dry enough, flip it back over and cook the first side
    very briefly again. Slide the galette out of the pan and keep
    it warm while you cook the remainder (the first one may not
    come out too well but the rest, once the pan is really hot and
    seasoned, will be fine). Stack with pieces of baking paper in
    between each galette.

5   Place a galette on a plate. Put the filling of your choice in the
    centre and fold in the sides to form a square with the filling
    visible in the centre. If using cheese, make sure that's on top.
    Repeat with remaining galettes and serve straight away. Or,
    if you like your pancakes and filling really hot and crispy, fill
    and fold, then place on baking sheets and heat through in
    the oven at 180oC/Gas 4 for about 5 minutes.

FRENCH-STYLE SWEET CRÊPES

Favourite fillings are chocolate hazelnut spread (with or without sliced pears or raspberries); apple purée and vanilla ice cream, or slightly sweetened soft white cheese and sliced banana (and drizzled with hot chocolate sauce); or, for traditional crêpes suzette, fold the crêpes in quarters. Melt about 100g unsalted butter in the pan and add 4 tbsp clear honey, the grated zest and juice of a large orange and 2 tbsp orange liqueur or brandy and heat until bubbling, then bubble for several minutes until syrupy. Slide the pancakes into the pan and coat with the sauce. Warm 4 tbsp orange liqueur or brandy in a ladle or small saucepan. Pour over the pancakes and ignite. Shake the pan until the flames subside, then serve with whipped or clotted cream.

Makes about 10

450ml milk
2 eggs
175g plain flour
a pinch of salt
1½ tbsp clear honey
20g butter, melted
a little sunflower or groundnut oil for frying

1 Put all the ingredients except the melted butter and frying oil in the blender goblet in the order listed. Secure the lid.

2 Select Variable Speed 1. Switch on the machine and gradually increase to Variable Speed 10 (or maximum for your machine). Blend for 10 seconds. Stop and scrape down the sides to make sure no flour is sticking to the goblet. Secure the lid again.

3 Select Variable Speed 1. Switch on the machine and blend a further 10 seconds.

4 Pour in the butter through the plug in the lid. Replace the plug and blend for a further 5 seconds.

5 Heat a little oil in a 23cm non-stick frying pan. Pour off the excess and reserve for the next crêpe. Pour in enough batter to swirl round the pan and just coat the base. Fry until golden underneath, the top is set and the edges are browning. Flip the pancake over – it should look quite lacy – and fry the other side. If not dry and crisp enough, flip back over briefly to dry out. Slide it out of the pan and keep it warm whilst cooking the remainder, layering each one with a piece of baking paper in between. Fill and serve as required (see intro).

TRADITIONAL PANCAKES

These can be served either savoury or sweet. I like to make smaller ones but you can, of course use a 20–23cm diameter frying pan, if you prefer. Popular savoury fillings include canned tuna mixed with sweetcorn in cheese sauce (see page 99 for the sauce); sautéed strips of red, yellow and green pepper and sliced courgettes and sliced onions, tossed with a little passata and a good sprinkling of Cajun spices (see page 160 or use shop-bought); sliced mixed mushrooms, sautéed in butter, then stirred into crème fraîche and flavoured with fresh thyme, which, once rolled, are packed into flameproof dish, topped with grated cheese and grilled until golden and bubbling. Sweet pancakes are best simply served drizzled with clear honey or maple syrup with a squeeze of lemon juice but you could use any of the sweet French crêpe ideas (see page 178) too.

Makes about 14

300ml milk
1 large egg
115g plain flour
a pinch of salt
a little sunflower or groundnut oil, for frying

1 Put all the ingredients except the frying oil in the blender goblet in the order listed. Secure the lid.

2 Select Variable Speed 1. Switch on the machine and gradually increase to Variable Speed 10 (or maximum for your machine). Blend for 10 seconds. Stop, scrape down the sides to make sure no flour is sticking to the sides then blend a further 10 seconds. If time, leave to stand for 20 minutes, then whisk briefly with a fork.

3 Heat a little oil in a 17cm non-stick omelette pan until very hot, then pour off the excess. Pour in enough batter to swirl round the pan and just coat the base. Fry until golden underneath, flip over and fry the other side. If the pancake is not as crisp as you'd like, tip it back over and cook very briefly to dry out. Slide the pancake out of the pan and keep it warm while you cook the remainder. Serve as required.

PRAWN AND ASPARAGUS TEMPURA

Tempura batter is crisp and light. Use it for sticks of root vegetable (I blanch them briefly in boiling water, drain and dry them first) or courgettes, or for pieces of chicken or a selection of mixed fish as well as for this delicious combination.

Serves 4

4 tbsp cornflour
250g asparagus, trimmed and cut into 5cm lengths
240g raw king prawns, thawed, if frozen, and dried on
    kitchen paper
groundnut oil, for deep-frying

For the batter
200ml ice-cold sparkling mineral water
75g self-raising flour
75g cornflour
½ tsp salt

To serve
a crisp salad and wedges of lemon

1   Put the 4 tbsp cornflour in a large bowl. Toss the asparagus and prawns in it to coat completely. Tip out any excess cornflour.

2   Heat the oil for deep-frying until a cube of day-old bread browns in 30 seconds. While it is heating up, put the batter ingredients in the blender goblet. Secure the lid.

3   Select Variable Speed 1. Switch on the machine and increase to Variable Speed 10 (or maximum for your machine), then stop straight away.

4   Pour the batter over the asparagus and prawns. Toss to coat completely. Lift out pieces of asparagus and prawns one at a time and drop into the hot oil. Cook several pieces at a time but don't overcrowd the pan or the temperature of the oil will fall too much. Fry the tempura for a few minutes until crisp and golden. Remove with a slotted spoon and drain on kitchen paper. Keep it warm whilst cooking the remainder, reheating the oil in between.

5   Serve a mixture of asparagus and prawns for each person, with a crisp salad and a wedge of lemon to squeeze over.

POPOVERS

Use the same mixture for plain mini Yorkshire puddings, or heat oil in a shallow 18 x 28 cm baking tin and cook one large Yorkshire pudding in the same way (but it will take a little longer to cook through). You can wet-chop the onion in the blender goblet before you make the batter. Simply drop in the quartered onion, add enough water so it floats off the blades then pulse the machine a few times until finely chopped. Drain thoroughly in a colander before use.

Makes 12

For the batter
150ml milk
150ml water
2 eggs
115g plain flour
a pinch of salt

For the filling
sunflower or groundnut oil
1 onion, peeled and finely chopped
6 top-quality pork chipolata sausages, cut into bite-sized chunks
8–12 sage leaves, chopped
freshly ground black pepper

To serve
baked beans in tomato sauce, or Vegetable Gravy (see page 100), potatoes and a green vegetable

1 Put the batter ingredients in the blender in the order listed. Secure the lid.

2 Select Variable Speed 1. Switch on the machine and gradually increase to Variable Speed 10 (or maximum for your machine). Blend for 30 seconds. Leave the batter to stand in the blender goblet for 30 minutes–1 hour before use for best results.

3 Preheat the oven to 220°C/Gas 7. Put a teaspoon of oil in each of 12 sections of a muffin tin. Add the chopped onion, sausage pieces and sage. Place in the oven and bake for 5 minutes until sizzling.

4 Pulse the machine once, then pour the batter from the jug over the hot sausage mixture in the tins (it will almost but not quite fill the tins) Return to the oven and bake for about 20 minutes, or until well risen, crisp and golden. Serve hot with baked beans in tomato sauce, or gravy, potatoes and a green vegetable.

AMERICAN PANCAKES WITH MAPLE SYRUP

For a mega American-style breakfast, serve these fluffy pancakes with grilled bacon as well as the syrup (make sure it's 'real' maple syrup, not just a flavoured sugar syrup). You can use the same recipe but unsweetened to make little blinis (although they are usually made with yeast, these work very well and are much quicker to make). It will also make little dropped scones, simply use honey instead of maple syrup in the mix. For either, make the batter in the same way but pour in separate small amounts of batter at a time to make pancakes 3–4cm in diameter.

Makes 6

200ml milk
1 large egg
125g self-raising flour
a pinch of salt
2 tsp baking powder
2 tbsp maple syrup
sunflower or groundnut oil, for frying

To serve
real maple syrup

1 Put the ingredients in the blender goblet in the order listed. Secure the lid.

2 Select Variable Speed 1. Switch on the machine and gradually increase to Variable Speed 10 (or maximum for your machine). Blend for 10 seconds. Stop and scrape down the sides to make sure no flour is sticking to the goblet. Secure the lid again.

3 Select Variable Speed 1. Switch on the machine and gradually increase to variable speed 10 (maximum) again. Blend for a further 10 seconds.

4 Heat a little oil in a non-stick frying pan until very hot, then pour off the excess. Turn down the heat to moderate. Pour in enough batter to form a pancake about 15cm in diameter. Fry until golden underneath, puffing up and bubbles have risen and popped on the surface. Flip over and fry the other side briefly to brown. Slide the pancake out of the pan and keep it warm while you cook the remainder, layering each one with a piece of baking paper. Serve topped with maple syrup.

SPINACH, SUN-DRIED TOMATO AND GOATS' CHEESE FRITTATA

This makes a large frittata but you can, of course, use half the ingredients and cook in a smaller pan. Blending up the spinach in the mix gives a delicious flavour. Try other combinations with quick-cooking ingredients, such as courgettes, mushrooms, grated hard cheese and/or tomatoes.

Serves 4

8 eggs
100g fresh young spinach, well washed and drained
8 sun-dried tomato pieces
a good pinch of salt
freshly ground black pepper
2 tbsp olive oil
100g soft goats' cheese
8 torn basil leaves
6 stoned black olives, halved
6 baby plum tomatoes, halved

1 Put the eggs, spinach and sun-dried tomato pieces in the blender goblet and add the salt and a good grinding of pepper. Secure the lid.

2 Select Variable Speed 1. Switch on the machine and gradually increase to Variable Speed 3. Blend for 5 seconds only, no longer, just until the spinach is chopped.

3 Heat the oil in a 23cm non-stick, frying pan. Pour in the egg mixture and fry, lifting the edge gently and tilting the pan to allow the uncooked mixture to run underneath, for about 3 minutes until almost set – still wet on top but browning underneath

4 Preheat the grill. Dot small spoonfuls of the cheese all over the surface of the frittata. Scatter with torn basil leaves, the olives and plum tomatoes then place under the grill for a few minutes until flecked golden and just firm. Leave to cool for 5 minutes to allow the flavours to develop, then serve cut into wedges and serve straight from the pan.

HERB TORTILLA

Spanish tortillas are usually made with thinly sliced potato but preparing it this way takes much less work! It is equally delicious hot or cold. I've used parsley and thyme but you could use sage and chive for a change.

Serves 4

1 onion, peeled and quartered
1 large potato (about 250g), cut in rough chunks
2 tbsp olive oil
a knob of butter
4 sprigs of curly-leaf parsley
a small handful of thyme, woody stems removed
6 eggs
salt and freshly ground black pepper

1 Put the onion and potatoes and onion in the blender goblet. Half-fill with water to float the ingredients off the blades. Secure the lid.
2 Select Variable Speed 1. Switch on the machine and pulse 2–3 times to chop. Drain thoroughly and dry on kitchen paper.

3   Heat 1 tbsp of the oil and the butter in a non-stick, 23cm frying pan. Add the potato and onion and stir-fry for 4–5 minutes over a medium heat until softening. Reduce the heat to low, spread out the mixture, cover and cook a further 5–10 minutes, stirring occasionally, until completely soft but not brown.

4   Rinse out the blender goblet and add the herbs. Break in the eggs, add a good pinch of salt and plenty of pepper. Secure the lid. Select Variable Speed 1 then increase to Variable Speed 4 and blend for 5 seconds until the herbs are chopped.

5   Pour the mixture into the pan. Stir well to incorporate the egg with the potato mixture then cook over a fairly low heat, lifting the edges as it sets to allow the runny egg to flow underneath until almost set, about 5 minutes. Loosen the edges and place a plate over the pan. Tip the tortilla out onto the plate then slide it back in, browned-side up. Fry for a minute or two more until brown underneath and set. Serve warm or cold cut in wedges.

CHAPTER 7

CHAPTER 7
SAUCES, RELISHES AND DRESSINGS

Your high-speed blender can make short work of all the accompaniments you need to moisten and flavour dishes for serving. You can finely chop salsas, process relishes until perfectly blended, make beautiful thick and thin sauces and cook them, too, as well as blend mayonnaise and other salad dressings to velvety unctuousness. Not only that, it takes a fraction of the time it would take conventionally!

MEXICAN TOMATO, ONION AND CORIANDER SALSA

Pico di gallo, also called *salsa fresco*, is served all over Mexico. You'll find it on the table in restaurants served with tortilla chips to scoop it up while you await your order. It goes brilliantly as an accompaniment to chilli con carne or any grilled spiced chicken meat or fish, too. Try it to top jacket baked potatoes with a dollop of soured cream as well.

Serves 4-6

2 tomatoes, quartered
1 small onion, peeled and quartered
a handful of coriander leaves
juice of 1 lime
1 jalapeño pepper, stalk removed (but leave in the seeds)
salt and freshly ground black pepper

1 Put all the ingredients in the blender goblet. Secure the lid.
2 Select Variable Speed 4. Switch on the machine and pulse a few times until chopped fairly finely, using the tamper, if necessary, to push the ingredients onto the blades.
3 Scoop into a serving bowl. Either serve immediately or, for more flavour, cover with clingfilm and chill in the fridge for an hour first.

HOLLANDAISE

My Hollandaise uses whole eggs (so no waste!). The result is a smooth pouring sauce, perfect to serve with fish, eggs or asparagus. It's not as thick as when made conventionally but way less effort!

Serves 4

115g butter
2 eggs
2 tsp chopped tarragon (optional)
1 tbsp lemon juice
a good pinch of salt
freshly ground black pepper
¼ tsp cayenne

1   Melt the butter in a measuring jug in the microwave or in a small saucepan, ideally with a lip for easy pouring.
2   Break the eggs into the blender goblet. Add the tarragon, if using, 1 tbsp lemon juice and the seasonings.
3   Select Variable Speed 1. Switch on the machine and gradually increase to Variable Speed 5 and blend for 10 seconds. Remove the lid plug and with the machine running, gradually add the melted butter in a slow trickle. Continue running the machine until the mixture thickens – about 1 minute. Use straight away.

MAYONNAISE

Like my Hollandaise, I use whole eggs as I hate having egg whites lurking in the fridge and they are not that useful unless you want to make loads of meringues or for glazing some pastry. I prefer to use sunflower oil for mayonnaise as it has a more neutral flavour but you could use half sunflower oil, half olive oil or all olive oil if you prefer. Should you add the oil too quickly and the mixture doesn't thicken, pour it out of the machine, break in another egg then, with the machine running as before, gradually trickle in the thin mayonnaise and it will become thick and unctuous.

Makes about 450ml

2 eggs
⅛ tsp made English mustard
⅛ tsp salt
a good pinch of white pepper
250ml sunflower oil
4 tsp lemon juice, or to taste

1   Break the eggs into the blender goblet and add the mustard, salt and pepper. Secure the lid.

2   Select Variable Speed 1.Gradually increase to Variable Speed 5 and run the machine for 10 seconds.

3   Remove the plug from the lid. Switch on the machine again at Variable Speed 5, and gradually add half the oil in a very thin trickle though the lid. The mixture will become very thick. Don't add the oil too quickly or the mixture won't thicken. Add the lemon juice and blend briefly. Continue adding the remaining oil, again in a thin trickle. Blend until thick, vey pale and glossy. Stop the machine, taste and add more seasoning or lemon juice as necessary, pulsing the machine once or twice to mix in.

4   Spoon into a clean screw-topped jar and store in the fridge. Use within 2–3 weeks.

FRESH TOMATO AND BASIL SAUCE

This is a great sauce to make, especially in summer if you have a glut of home-grown tomatoes. I always choose tomatoes still on the vine when buying as they definitely have a better flavour. Use it to stir through pasta, to spread on pizza bases before adding cheese or other toppings, serve it with eggs or Mediterranean vegetables or with grilled fish, chicken or meat. For a more concentrated sauce, tip it into a saucepan after step 2, bring to the boil and boil rapidly for several minutes until reduced to the consistency you require. It will keep in the fridge for 3 days or can be frozen for up to 6 months.

Makes about 450ml

400g tomatoes
3 tbsp dried onions
3 tbsp tomato purée
1 tsp clear honey
1 garlic clove, peeled
6 large basil leaves
salt and freshly ground black pepper

1   Put all the ingredients in the blender goblet in the order listed, adding just a little salt and plenty of pepper. Secure the lid.
2   Select Variable Speed 1. Switch on the machine and gradually increase to Variable Speed 10 (or maximum for your machine). Using the tamper to press the ingredients on the blades, if necessary, blend for 30 seconds or until smooth.
3   Taste and add more seasoning, if necessary. If you want to serve the sauce hot straight away, continue to blend on Variable Speed 10 for 5 minutes until the goblet feels piping hot and steam escapes when the lid is removed. Use as required.

BLENDER WHITE SAUCE

If you can, heat the milk briefly in the microwave first as the sauce will cook a lot quicker in the blender with warm milk (although you can make it with cold). The sauce is suitable for pouring over vegetables for a gratin, for mixing with fish for a fish pie, or using to cover lasagne or other pasta that is going to be baked. If you are just serving the sauce as an accompaniment, you may detect a slight 'floury' taste as the sauce isn't boiled long enough to cook out the starch completely in the blender (but it will be beautifully glossy). For a lasagne for four people, you will need to make double the quantity.

Makes about 300ml

300ml warm milk
4 tbsp plain flour
a large knob of butter
a large pinch of salt
freshly ground black pepper
½ tsp dried mixed herbs

1   Put all the ingredients in the blender goblet in the order listed. Secure the lid.
2   Select Variable Speed 1. Switch on the machine and gradually increase to Variable Speed 10 (or maximum for your machine). Blend for 5 minutes until thickened, glossy and the goblet feels really hot to the touch. Use as required.

Cheese Sauce
Add 2 large handfuls of grated strong Cheddar or other melting hard cheese when the sauce is cooked and blend a further 30 seconds until melted and incorporated.

VEGETABLE GRAVY

This is a useful gravy to whip up when you need something moist to go with anything from sausages or Popovers (see page 84) to chops, or even haggis! For special occasions I add a splash of brandy to the sauce as it really enhances the flavour. If you are not using reduced-salt soy sauce, use a tablespoonful only or it will be too salty.

Serves 4

450ml boiling vegetable stock
3 tbsp instant oat cereal
1½ tbsp reduced-salt soy sauce
1 carrot, peeled and cut in rough chunks
2 mushrooms, preferably chestnut
2 tbsp dried onions
½ tsp dried mixed herbs
salt and freshly ground black pepper

1 Put the ingredients in the blender goblet in the order listed. Secure the lid.
2 Select Variable Speed 1. Gradually increase to Variable Speed 10 (or maximum for your machine) and blend for 3–4 minutes or until piping hot and thickened slightly. Taste and add more seasoning or soy sauce if necessary. Use as required.

CLASSIC FRENCH DRESSING

This is ideal drizzled over fresh green salad leaves then gently tossed, to moisten any combination of salad vegetables or to dress rice or pasta salads. Store it in the fridge in a clean screw-topped jar then just shake well before use each time you need some.

Makes about 200ml

150ml extra-virgin olive oil
2 tsp Dijon mustard
1 tbsp clear honey
a pinch of salt
plenty of freshly ground black pepper
3 tbsp red or white wine vinegar

1 Put all the ingredients in the blender goblet. Secure the lid.
2 Select Variable Speed 1. Switch on the machine and gradually increase to Variable Speed 10 (or maximum for your machine) and blend for 10 seconds until emulsified and thickened slightly. Pour into a screw-topped jar and use as required.

FRESH FRUIT COULIS

A coulis is great made in this high-speed blender, particularly with berries, as it almost eliminates the seeds so you don't need to sieve it. If using a soft fruit, like mango, there's no need to process quite so long, just blend until smooth and thick. I like to use thick honey for this but you could use thin if you prefer.

Makes about 300ml

250g fresh raspberries, blackcurrants, mango flesh or
    strawberries
2 tbsp thick honey or to taste
1 tsp lemon or lime juice, or to taste

1   If necessary prepare the fruit: hull strawberries, remove blackcurrants from their stalks with the prongs of a fork, or pick over raspberries.
2   Put the prepared fruit in the blender goblet. Add the honey and lemon or lime juice. Secure the lid.
3   Select Variable Speed 1. Switch on the machine and gradually increase to Variable Speed 10 (or maximum for your machine). Blend for 20–30 seconds or until smooth, using the tamper to press down ingredients if necessary.
4   Taste and add more honey or citrus juice if needed. Blend again briefly to mix in. If not using immediately, spoon into a sealable container and store in the fridge. It will keep a few days.

CHAPTER 8
SAVOURY PATTIES
AND KEBABS

Your high-speed blender can process mixtures to turn into every sort of delectable savoury 'cake' you could wish for from burgers to kebabs. There's hardly any effort required. However, don't expect your machine to behave like a mincer or food processor. It is so quick and powerful that it chops very finely which means the mixture sticks together really well without having to use binders, such as egg, for most dishes. If you want a granular texture, use minced meat for any of the recipes (as I have for the steak burgers to show you how to do it). Chop any onion or vegetable first then add the minced meat with the remaining ingredients and blend on Variable Speed 4 or 5 for a few seconds only until thoroughly mixed, using the tamper to press the mixture onto the blades so it mixes quickly. Don't over-blend or you will end up with paste!

STEAK BURGERS

Meaty, mighty and flavoursome. Because I like the chunkier texture of minced meat for these, I have used ready-minced steak here but you could process your own diced lean steak for a smoother-textured burger.

Serves 4

1 small onion, peeled and quartered
1–2 tsp Dijon or made English mustard
¼ tsp salt
freshly ground black pepper
500g lean minced steak
a little sunflower oil, for frying

To serve
burger buns, shredded lettuce, sliced tomatoes, dill pickle
   slices, mustard and ketchup

1 Place the onion and mustard in the blender goblet. Secure the lid.
2 Select Variable Speed 5. Switch on the machine. Pulse twice to roughly chop. Scrape down and pulse once or twice again until fairly finely chopped.
3 Add the beef, salt and plenty of pepper. Secure the lid. Switch on the machine and increase speed to Variable Speed 4–5. Use the tamper to press the meat onto the blades and process for 5 seconds until the bottom third of the mixture is brown and the onion is well mixed in. Tip out of the machine into a bowl and use your hands to work it together, mixing the red mince in with the browner, blended mixture. Shape into 4 thick, flat cakes about 10cm diameter. Make a slight hole in the centre of each with your finger (it will close up as they cook and helps prevent the burgers from shrinking).
4 Preheat the grill or a griddle pan. Brush the burgers on both sides with oil and grill or griddle for 3-4 minutes on each side until browned and cooked through. Serve in burger buns with shredded lettuce, sliced tomatoes, dill pickles, mustard and ketchup.

MINI CHICKEN MEATBALLS

These fiery little balls can be served as a nibble with some soured cream to dip with aperitifs, or packed into wholemeal pitta breads with some shredded lettuce and guacamole (see page 64) as a light lunch or supper. Alternatively, try the balls tossed in hot fresh Tomato Sauce (see page 98) and piled onto spaghetti then topped with the plenty of grated Parmesan and served with a crisp salad for a more substantial meal.

Makes 20

1 garlic clove, peeled
1 shallot, peeled and halved
½ tsp dried chilli flakes (or to taste)
1½ tsp za'atar (or ½ tsp ground cumin and 1 tsp dried oregano)
½ tsp salt
freshly ground black pepper
350g skinless chicken breast or thigh, cut into chunks
2– 3 tbsp plain flour
olive oil

1   Put the garlic and shallot in the blender goblet. Secure the lid. Select Variable Speed 1. Switch on the machine and pulse once to chop. Add the chilli, za'atar, salt and some pepper.

2   Remove the bung from the lid. Select Variable 1. Switch on the machine, turn up to Variable 6 and drop in the pieces of chicken one at a time to mince. Use the tamper towards the end to press the last pieces onto the blades. Stop the machine as soon as they are all finely chopped.

3   Mix the flour with a little salt and pepper on a plate. With wet hands, shape the mixture into 20 small balls and roll in the seasoned flour.

4   Shallow-fry the balls in a little hot oil for 4– 5 minutes, turning occasionally until golden brown and cooked through. Drain on kitchen paper. Serve hot.

QUICK SALMON FISHCAKES

Fishcakes are a staple food in many households. They are so quick easy and economical to make at home – particularly if you use canned salmon. It is particularly nutritious, too, as the bones are whizzed up with the fish and that gives you a great whack of extra calcium into the diet. You can substitute canned sardines or tuna for the salmon for a change, too. They are also good served with the Fresh Tomato and Basil Sauce (see page 98) and green beans.

Serves 4

2 large potatoes, scrubbed
2 spring onions, trimmed and roughly cut up
a handful of parsley, stalks removed
213g can pink salmon, drained and skin removed (leave the
    bones)
2 tbsp Thai fish sauce
freshly ground black pepper
50g frozen peas
3–4 tbsp plain flour
1 egg, beaten
8 tbsp panko breadcrumbs
sunflower or groundnut oil, for frying

For the dressing
3 tbsp crème fraîche
1½ tbsp dill and anchovy pesto (see page 66) or a bought
    green pesto

To serve
sprouting broccoli or a mixed salad

1 Prick the potatoes all over with a fork. Place on the turntable of the microwave and cook on HIGH for 8–9 minutes until soft. When cool enough to handle, cut in large chunks. Alternatively, cut into chunks and boil in water for about 15 minutes until tender, then drain.

2 Place the potato in the blender goblet with the spring onions, parsley, salmon, fish sauce and lots of pepper. Secure the lid.

3 Select Variable Speed 1. Switch on the machine and gradually increase to Variable Speed 5. Blend for 20–30 seconds, using the tamper to press down the food onto the blades, and stopping and scraping down the sides as necessary until well mixed and fairly smooth and soft.

4 Scoop into a bowl. Add the peas and mix in. Line a baking tray with baking paper.

5 Mix the flour with a little salt and pepper on a plate. Beat the egg on a second plate and put the breadcrumbs on a third one. Divide the mixture into eighths. Take an eighth on a spoon and drop into the seasoned flour. Toss gently to coat (it will be very soft), then dip on both sides in beaten egg then breadcrumbs, shaping it into a fishcake with your hands. Place on the prepared baking tray. Repeat with the remaining mixture. Chill until ready to cook.

6 Mix the crème fraîche and pesto together and chill until ready to serve.

7 Heat 5mm oil in a large frying pan and shallow-fry the fish cakes for about 3 minutes on each side until golden brown and hot through. Drain on kitchen paper. Serve with a dollop of the pesto dressing and sprouting broccoli or a mixed salad.

ALMOST FAGGOTS

Faggots are a traditional British dish in which minced pigs' offal is mixed with breadcrumbs and herbs and, traditionally, is wrapped in the pig's caul – the fat membrane that surrounds a pig's stomach – which, when baked in the oven, gave a lovely edible, golden skin on the moist, flavoursome patties. Here I've made a similar tasty mixture using pork and pig's liver but blended it – so it's quite smooth – and wrapped it in streaky bacon to bake. Because I use an egg to keep the liver moist when cooked, it is a very sticky mixture to work with but don't worry, when baked it firms up beautifully!

Serves 4-5

For the faggots
1 onion, peeled and quartered
12 large sage leaves (or 1 tsp dried)
1 egg
2 slices wholemeal bread, cut into cubes
450g diced pork
250g pigs' liver, diced
a good grating of fresh nutmeg
¾ tsp salt
freshly ground black pepper
15g butter
8–10 rindless unsmoked streaky bacon rashers

For the gravy
3 tbsp plain flour
300ml beef stock
1 tbsp reduced-salt soy sauce

To serve
new potatoes, peas and a leafy green vegetable

1   Put the onion and sage in the blender goblet. Secure the lid.
2   Select Variable Speed 1. Switch on the machine and gradually increase to Variable Speed 5 and blend for a few seconds to chop. Add the egg, bread, pork, liver and seasonings. Secure the lid again and blend for 10 seconds, using the tamper to press the ingredients on the blades. Stop, use a spatula to turn the mixture over on the blades then secure the lid again. Select variable speed 1. Switch on and increase again to Variable Speed 5. Use the tamper again to press the mixture on the blades and blend until just processed, about a further 10 seconds. Scoop the very soft mixture into a bowl. Give it a stir again to make sure it's all evenly mixed.
3   Use the butter to grease liberally a shallow baking tin or dish, about 18cm x 25cm.
4   Stretch each bacon rasher with the back of a knife.
5   Preheat the oven to 180ºC/Gas 4. Use wet hands to take an eighth or 10th of the mixture and shape into a soft ball. Gently wrap a bacon rasher around it and place in one corner of the prepared baking tin or dish. Repeat with all the remaining mixture, packing the patties side by side in two rows. Pour 100ml water around. Cover with foil and bake for 30 minutes. Remove the foil, increase the oven temperature to 200ºC/Gas 6 and bake for a further 20-25 minutes to brown.
6   Put the flour in a small saucepan and stir in 3 tbsp water until smooth. Gradually blend in the stock then carefully pour in any liquid from the faggot dish. Add the soy sauce. Bring to the boil and cook for 2 minutes, stirring all the time. Taste and season as necessary.
7   Carefully transfer the faggots on to warm plates and spoon some gravy over. Serve with new potatoes, peas, a green vegetable and the rest of the gravy handed separately.

KOFTA KEBABS

I like to serve these spicy kebabs with a Greek-style salad too. Simply shred crisp lettuce and some white cabbage too if you like, and top with sliced tomatoes, cubes of cucumber, black olives, onion rings and some cubes of feta cheese. Sprinkle with dried oregano and dress with a drizzle of olive oil and red wine vinegar. Sprinkle with a pinch of salt and add a good grinding of black pepper.

Serves 4

For the kebabs
1 small onion, peeled
2 large garlic cloves, peeled
450g lean pork, lamb or beef
a small handful of coriander leaves
2 tsp ground cumin
2 tsp sweet paprika
½ tsp chilli powder
1 tsp dried oregano
salt and freshly ground black pepper
8 soaked wooden skewers
2 tbsp olive oil

For the Tzaziki
¼ cucumber, grated
200ml thick plain yoghurt
2 tsp dried mint
salt and pepper

To serve
plain boiled rice

1 Preheat the grill. Put all the ingredients except the skewers and olive oil in the blender goblet in the order listed. Secure the lid.

2 Select Variable Speed 1. Switch on the machine and gradually increase to Variable Speed 5. Using the tamper, press the meat onto the blades and blend for 5 seconds only. Stop the machine and use a spatula to turn some of the processed mixture over the unchopped meat. Secure the lid again. Switch on and increase to Variable 5 and use the tamper to press the meat on until just processed – about 10 seconds.

3 Scoop the mixture out onto a plate. Divide into eight equal pieces and shape each into a cylinder around a soaked wooden skewer, so they're about half the length of the sticks.

4 Brush with olive oil and place on the grill rack. Grill for 10-12 minutes, turning once until golden and cooked through.

5 Meanwhile, squeeze the grated cucumber to remove excess moisture. Mix with the yoghurt, mint and a little salt and pepper.

6 Serve the kebabs with plain rice and the tzaziki.

LAMB DONER KEBAB

Everyone's favourite late-night snack but it's so easy to make at home! Delicious, juicy slices of pressed minced meat flavoured with garlic, chilli and herbs. If you're really hungry, serve with potato wedges too. Any leftovers are delicious sliced cold with pickles. If you prefer, you can use ready-minced meat. Chop the onion at step 1 then add the meat and remaining ingredients and continue from step 2.

Serves 4

2 tbsp milk
1 garlic clove, peeled
1 banana shallot or small onion, peeled and cut into chunks
30g bread, cut in cubes
450g lean lamb, cubed
good pinch of chilli powder
1 tsp dried oregano
1 tsp dried mint
½ tsp salt
a good grinding of black pepper
a little sunflower oil

For the harissa mayonnaise
4 tbsp mayonnaise (see page 96 or use bought)
1 tbsp harissa paste

To serve
warm wholemeal pitta breads, shredded lettuce, sliced pickled gherkins, pickled turnip or pickled onion, a large mixed salad including avocado, olives, tomatoes and red onions

1   Preheat the oven to 180°C/Gas 4. Put the ingredients in the blender goblet in the order listed. Select Variable Speed 6. Switch on the machine then blend for 10-15 seconds, pressing the ingredients onto the blades with the tamper through the bung hole in the lid.

2   Scoop the mixture out of the machine. Shape it into a squat, fat loaf 10–12 cm diameter.

3   Place the loaf on a rack or small upturned plate set in a roasting tin. Brush with a little oil. Roast in the oven for 1 hour. Check halfway through cooking and baste with any juices in the pan or brush with a little more sunflower oil.

4   Remove from the oven, cover with foil and leave in a warm place to rest for 10 minutes whilst you mix the mayonnaise with the harissa paste, warm and split the pittas and prepare the salad ingredients.

5   Thinly slice the meat and serve in the pittas with some harissa mayonnaise, some shredded lettuce and pickles with a large mixed salad to accompany.

CHAPTER 9

THE BEST BAKES

Not only can you use your blender as a food processor to mix and combine mixtures ready for baking, but you can even make your own flour. Simply choose the grain – for instance wheat, spelt, barley, buckwheat, rye, oats, brown rice or millet. Tip them into the blender goblet and secure the lid. Select Variable Speed 1. Switch on the machine. Gradually increase to Variable Speed 10 (or maximum for your machine). Process for 1 minute until finely ground into flour. To make nut flour, put the nuts of your choice into the blender goblet. Secure the lid. Select Variable Speed 1 then gently pulse the machine (by switching on and off quickly) until ground as finely as you like. However, don't continue too long or you will release the oils in the nuts and end up with nut butter! Remember when making these recipes, the texture will be different from when you make by traditional methods – pastry and bread doughs are softer but behave beautifully when baked. Remember to always use a wet spatula to scoop any annoying stray bits of mixture out of the goblet. It's a skill that I've found has improved with much practice!

BEEF AND VEGETABLE PASTIES

Use this shortcrust to make any pies or tarts as well as these delicious pasties which make a wholesome mid-week treat. Spelt flour gives a delicious short result but is a little more difficult to handle. If you use plain flour you may need a little water. Make the pastry first so it has time to rest while you prepare the filling.

Serves 4

For the shortcrust pastry
300g spelt or plain flour, plus extra for dusting
¼ tsp salt
150g butter, cut in cubes
4 tbsp cold water

For the filling
½ leek or 1 banana shallot, peeled and cut in small chunks
1 carrot, peeled and cut in small chunks
1 turnip, peeled and cut in small chunks
250g lean minced steak
½ tsp dried mixed herbs
2 tbsp reduced-salt soy sauce
freshly ground black pepper
1 egg, beaten, to glaze

1 Put the flour and salt in the blender goblet. Secure the lid. Select Variable Speed 6. Blend briefly, then stop the machine. A hole will appear in the flour. Add the butter and water. Select Variable 1. Switch on the machine and gradually increase to Variable 10 (or maximum for your machine), using the tamper to press the butter onto the blades. Blend for about 10 seconds until a soft dough is formed.

2 Scoop out of the machine (the dough round the blades will come away fairly cleanly with a spatula – it just takes a few seconds). Wrap the pastry in clingfilm and chill for at least 30 minutes.

3 Meanwhile, make the filling. Put the vegetables in the blender. Secure the lid. Select Variable Speed 1. Switch on the machine and pulse several times to chop the vegetables fairly finely. Tip into a bowl and mix in the minced steak, herbs, soy sauce and plenty of seasoning.

4 Preheat the oven to 200°C/Gas 6 and line a baking sheet with baking paper. Divide the pastry into quarters. Roll out each quarter on a floured surface to an 18cm diameter circle.

5 Divide the filling amongst the centres. Moisten the edges with water. Add 1 tbsp water to each pile of filling. Draw the pastry up over the filling and press together all along to seal. Crimp this edge between the finger and thumb to give an attractive finish. Check there are no cracks or the juices will run out as they cook.

6 Transfer the pasties to the prepared baking sheet. Brush all over with beaten egg to glaze, making sure you give a good coating to the seamed edges (and, if you do find a crack, brush the 'mend' liberally with the beaten egg to help seal it).

7 Bake in the oven for 40–45 minutes until a rich golden brown and the filling is cooked through. Check after 30 minutes and cover loosely with foil if over-browning. Serve hot or cold.

LEEK, APPLE AND BACON RAISED PIE

You can use this recipe to make a traditional pork pie with a minced pork and herb filling using your machine to chop the pork (see Kofta Kebabs, page 112) or use minced pork. Sausagemeat would also be good. Raised pies are not difficult to make, but look very impressive for a buffet or festive treat. In this pie there isn't much room for jelly when cooked but if you want to add a little to the cooked and cooled pie, dissolve 1 tsp powdered gelatine in 6 tbsp chicken stock. Use a plastic syringe to inject as much as you can through the steam hole in the pastry lid, then chill the pie again to allow it to set.

Serves 4-6

For the hot water crust pastry
300g plain flour, plus extra for dusting
¾ tsp salt
100g lard
150ml water

For the filling
1 leek (about 160g), trimmed and cut into chunks
1 small red eating apple, quartered and cored
6 large sage leaves
180g thick smoked bacon rashers, roughly cut up
freshly ground black pepper
1 egg, beaten, to glaze

To serve
a variety of pickles

1 Put the flour and salt in the blender goblet. Secure the lid. Select Variable Speed 1. Switch on the machine and gradually increase to Variable Speed 6, then switch off.

2 Put the lard and water in a small pan and heat until the lard melts. Bring to the boil. Pour into the blender goblet through the bung hole in the lid. Select Variable Speed 1. Switch on the machine and gradually increase to Variable Speed 4. Use the tamper to stir the mix a bit until a ball forms, then switch off straight away.

3 Tip the dough out of the machine, using a wet spatula to help, if necessary. Knead gently until smooth, then cut off one-third of the dough and wrap it in clingfilm, then a tea towel to keep it warm. Roll out the remainder on a lightly floured surface to 3–4mm thick and use to line a 500g loaf tin (preferably silicone but, at least, a good non-stick metal one. If using a metal tin, line with a strip of double thickness foil that stands up either end by about 5cm, to allow for easy releasing and grease the foil), making sure there are no cracks in the pastry when pressed all round and that the layer of pastry is even, so press right to the corners. Leave to set while preparing the filling.

4 Put the leek, apple, sage and bacon into the blender goblet (no need to wash the goblet first). Add a good grinding of pepper. Secure the lid. Select Variable Speed 1. Switch on the machine and gradually increase to Variable Speed 4 or 5. Use the tamper to press the meat onto the blades. Blend until all is chopped and looks like coarse sausagemeat. Scoop the mixture into the pastry-lined tin – it should be very full. Level the surface.

5   Preheat the oven to 200°C/Gas 6. Roll out the reserved pastry to a rectangle for a lid. Brush the edges with water and place the lid in position, trimming to fit. Make a small hole in the centre to allow steam to escape. Crimp the edge all round between the finger and thumb. Make leaves out of pastry trimmings. Brush the top with beaten egg, place the leaves on top to decorate. Brush again with beaten egg. Place on a baking sheet. Bake in the oven for 30 minutes until golden. Cover loosely with foil, turn down the heat to 180°C/Gas 4 and bake for a further 25 minutes to cook the filling and pastry completely. Remove from the oven and leave to cool in the tin, then chill until ready to serve.

6   Carefully remove the tin. If you are using silicone, it should pop out (but handle gently). If you are using a metal tin, loosen the edge with a round-bladed knife, then use the foil tags to help lift the pie out. Serve sliced with pickles.

CUT-AND-COME-AGAIN ROSEMARY COOKIES

This dough will keep wrapped in the fridge for up to 10 days. It can be frozen for up to 6 months, too.

Makes about 30

1 egg
1 tsp natural vanilla extract or paste
2 tsp chopped rosemary leaves
115g butter, softened
150g golden caster sugar
200g plain flour
25g cornflour
1 tsp baking powder

1　Put the egg, vanilla, rosemary, butter and sugar in the blender goblet. Secure the lid.

2　Select Variable Speed 1. Switch on the machine and gradually increase to Variable Speed 10 (or maximum for your machine). Blend for 20 seconds until smooth.

3　Sift the flour, cornflour and baking powder together. Add to the blender goblet. Select Variable Speed 1. Switch on the machine and gradually increase to Variable Speed 6, using the tamper to push down the ingredients onto the blades until a soft paste has formed.

4　Lay 2 sheets of clingfilm on the work surface. Remove the paste from the goblet, using a wet spatula to scoop it out. Divide the mixture in half and shape each into a fat sausage about 5cm diameter. Wrap securely and chill for several hours until firm.

5　Preheat the oven to190°C/Gas 5. Unwrap the dough and cut into slices about 5mm thick. Arrange a little apart on baking sheets lined with baking paper. Bake for about 12 minutes until golden. Cool slightly then transfer to a wire rack to cool completely and become crisp. Store in an airtight container.

CHOCOLATE ÉCLAIRS

Choux pastry can be made into éclairs, like here, or small balls – profiteroles – which can be filled with savoury mixtures, such as flavoured cream cheese, or mayonnaise and chopped prawns or, of course, the usual dessert option of filling with cream and topping with chocolate sauce. You can use the same mixture to pipe bigger rounds for cream buns (and fill with cream and fresh berries). I cheat and use a Belgian chocolate spread for the topping for my éclairs but you can use a glacé icing with icing sugar and cocoa or melted chocolate (or a little instant coffee powder), mixed to a thick cream with a dash of water.

Makes about 10

For the choux pastry
150ml water
50g butter
65g plain flour
a pinch of salt
1 very large egg, beaten

To finish
150ml double cream, whipped
3–4 tbsp dark Belgian chocolate spread

1 Put the water and butter in a saucepan and heat gently until the butter melts.

2 Meanwhile, put the flour and salt in the blender goblet. Secure the lid. Select Variable Speed 1. Switch on the machine and switch off again.

3 When the butter has melted, bring to the boil. Pour into the goblet. Secure the lid. Select Variable Speed 1. Switch on the machine and gradually increase to Variable Speed 6. Blend for 10 seconds. Stop and scrape down the sides, then blend briefly again. The mixture will leave the sides of the goblet.

4 Pour in about half the egg through the hole in the lid. Select Variable Speed 1. Switch on the machine and increase to Variable Speed 10 (or maximum for your machine). Blend for a few seconds until thick and smooth. Add the remaining egg and blend again – the mixture should be smooth and glossy but still hold its shape, with a swirl in the centre of the goblet.

5 Preheat the oven to 220ºC/Gas 7 and line a baking sheet with baking paper. Use the mixture to fill a piping bag fitted with a large plain nozzle. Pipe 15cm sausage shapes a little apart onto the prepared baking sheet. Bake for 10 minutes until risen and browning, turn down the oven to 180ºC/Gas 4 and bake a further 20 minutes until crisp and golden. Transfer to a wire rack to cool.

6 Make a slit in the side of each éclair and fill with the whipped cream. Gently spread the tops with the chocolate spread. Chill until ready to serve.

YOGHURT SCONES

These are plain scones to use with sweet or savoury toppings. For sweet ones, add 1 tbsp clear honey with the yoghurt. For cheese scones, add 75g grated mature Cheddar and 2 tsp celery seeds to the mix with the flour. The trick is to process just until a rough dough is beginning to form – it will still be lumpy and a bit crumbly. Don't over-process or the results will be tough.

Makes 8

150ml plain yoghurt
40g soft butter or butter spread
a pinch of salt
115g plain flour
115g wholemeal flour
4 tsp baking powder
a little extra yoghurt or some milk, to glaze

To serve
butter

1   Preheat the oven to 220ºC/Gas 7 and line a baking sheet with baking paper.

2   Put the yoghurt, butter, and salt in the blender goblet. Mix the flours and baking powder together and tip in. Secure the lid. Select Variable Speed 1. Switch on the machine and gradually increase to Variable Speed 6 and blend for 10 seconds until a rough ball of crumbly dough has formed Don't over-mix.

3   Remove from the blender, using a wet spatula to remove any dough stuck round the blades, briefly shape into a ball and pat out on a lightly floured surface to about 2cm thick. Cut about 8 scones, using a 5cm cutter, re-kneading any trimmings to make the last couple of scones. Place on the prepared baking sheet and brush the tops with a little extra yoghurt or milk to glaze.

4   Bake for 12 minutes, or until risen, golden and the bases sound hollow when tapped. Cool slightly on a wire rack and serve warm spread with butter. Store any remainder in an airtight container. Best served warm.

NUT AND MULTI-SEED LOAF

This moist packed-with-nutrients bread has a wonderful mix of flavours and uses rye and wholemeal flour but you could just use wholemeal of you prefer. It's great simply sliced with butter or served with cheese but it is also very good toasted for breakfast (have a banana too and you're set up for the day).

Makes 1 large loaf

50g walnut pieces
2 tsp caraway seeds
350g strong wholemeal bread flour
100g rye flour, plus a little for dusting
1 tsp salt
1 tbsp dried milk powder
1 tbsp easy-blend dried yeast
1 tbsp walnut or sunflower oil
3 tbsp clear honey
1 egg
300ml warm water
3 tbsp pumpkin seeds
3 tbsp sunflower seeds
3 tbsp sesame seeds
a little milk, for brushing

1   Put the nuts, caraway seeds, flours, salt, milk powder and yeast in the blender goblet. Secure the lid.
2   Select Variable Speed 1. Switch on the machine and gradually increase to Variable Speed 6. Blend for about 10 seconds until a hole appears in the centre of the mixture.

3 Add the oil, honey, egg and warm water. Secure the lid again. Switch on the machine and gradually increase the speed to Variable Speed 10 (or maximum for your machine) and blend for 10 seconds.

4 To knead the dough, remove the lid and, using the spatula, draw the dough away from the sides into the centre. Select Variable Speed 10 and pulse the machine 4 or 5 times (by switching on and off quickly). Repeat the scraping and pulsing 4 more times, letting the machine rest briefly in between. Add the seeds before scraping down the sides and pulse a few times to start to combine the seeds into the dough and to lift it off the blades. Tip out onto a well-floured surface, using a wet spatula to remove any dough stuck to the blades. The dough will be quite sticky.

5 Lightly oil a 900g loaf tin. Knead the dough briefly to work in the seeds more evenly, then shape into an oblong and place in the tin. Cover the tin loosely with lightly oiled clingfilm and leave in a warm place for about 1 hour or until it reaches top of the tin.

6 Preheat the oven to 200°C/Gas 6. Brush top of the loaf very lightly with milk and sprinkle evenly with rye flour. Bake for about 40 minutes, covering loosely with foil halfway through cooking to prevent over-browning, until risen, crusty-brown and the base sounds hollow when turned out and tapped. Cool on a wire rack for at least 30 minutes before slicing.

BLUEBERRY AND ORANGE MUFFINS

I make the mixture with some dried blueberries, then throw in a few whole fresh ones to each muffin before baking to impart a gorgeous juiciness. Again, I haven't used added sugar, just the lovely flavour of the fruits to give a hint of sweetness (there's no need to core the apple, by the way). They are delicious on their own or warm for breakfast with a little butter. For those with a sweeter tooth, add 2 tbsp clear honey with the eggs. Duck eggs are brilliant for baking as the whites have more protein than hens' eggs, which gives a lovely rise in muffins and cakes.

Makes 12

3 tbsp apple juice
1 red eating apple, quartered
75g stoned dates, chopped
2 large hens' eggs or 2 duck eggs
4 tbsp sunflower oil
finely grated zest and juice of 1 orange
1 tsp ground cinnamon
150g plain flour
150g wholemeal flour
2 tsp bicarbonate of soda
75g dried blueberries
100g fresh blueberries

1   Preheat the oven to 180ºC/Gas 4 and line 12 sections of a muffin tin with paper cases. Put the apple juice, apple quarters and dates in the blender goblet. Secure the lid.

2   Select Variable Speed 1. Switch on the machine and gradually increase to Variable Speed 10 (or maximum for your machine). Blend for 30 seconds until smooth, using the tamper if necessary to push the ingredients onto the blades.

3   Add the eggs, oil, orange zest and juice and the cinnamon. Secure the lid again and select Variable Speed 1. Switch on the machine and gradually increase to Variable Speed 10 (maximum) for 10 seconds.

4   Mix the flour with the bicarbonate of soda and dried blueberries. Select Variable Speed 1. Switch on the machine and gradually increase to Variable Speed 5, using the tamper to push the mixture on the blades. Blend for about 20 seconds.

5   Quickly spoon the mixture into the cases. Add 4 or 5 fresh blueberries to each muffin, then push them down into the mixture. Bake for about 20 minutes, or until risen, golden and springy to the touch. Cool on a wire rack.

RAPID BANANA BREAD

I've been making banana bread for years as it's the perfect way to use up those blackening fruit in the bowl that no one wants to eat (though they are fine in a smoothie too!). In the high-speed blender it takes literally a couple of minute to prepare! You can use 275g plain flour and omit the bran if you prefer.

Makes a 900g loaf

5 small very ripe bananas (or 3 larger ones), peeled
3 tbsp clear honey
1 tsp bicarbonate of soda
1 tsp ground cinnamon
1 large hens' egg or a duck egg
4 tbsp sunflower oil
265g self-raising flour
10g oat or wheat bran

To serve
butter (optional)

1   Preheat the oven to 180ºC/Gas 4 and grease a 900g loaf tin (or use a silicone one and then there is no need to grease).

2   Put the bananas, honey, bicarbonate of soda, cinnamon, egg and oil in the blender goblet. Secure the lid. Select Variable Speed 1. Switch on the machine and gradually increase to Variable Speed 10 (or maximum for your machine). Blend for 10 seconds.

3   Add the flour and bran. Secure the lid again. Select Variable Speed 1, using the tamper to press the flour onto the blades (in a sort of stirring motion), switch on the machine and increase to Variable Speed 6. Blend for about 5 seconds until mixed.

4   Scoop into the prepared tin, using a wet spatula to scrape out the bits from the sides and beneath the blades of the machine (this is the longest bit!). Bake in the oven for 40 minutes until well risen and brown and a skewer inserted in the centre comes out clean. Cool slightly, remove from the tin and cool on a wire rack. Serve sliced, with butter, if liked.

PERFECT PIZZAS

These are simple cheese and tomato pizzas but you could, of course, add any other toppings of your choice before the cheese. I like to serve mine topped with a handful of fresh rocket but it's not compulsory! You can also freeze half the dough for another day, if you prefer.

Makes 2 large pizzas

170g strong wholemeal bread flour
200g strong white bread flour
1 tbsp easy-blend dried yeast
½ tsp salt
2 tbsp olive oil, plus extra for greasing and drizzling
2 tsp clear honey
250ml lukewarm water
cornmeal, for dusting

For the topping
10 tbsp fresh Tomato Sauce (see page 98) or bottled passata
2 small handfuls of basil leaves
4 tbsp grated Parmesan
250g fresh Mozzarella, torn or sliced in pieces
freshly ground black pepper

To serve
2 large handfuls of fresh rocket (optional)

1   Put the flours, yeast and salt in the blender goblet. Secure the lid. Select Variable Speed 1. Switch on the machine and gradually increase to Variable Speed 6. Run the machine for a few seconds until a hole appears in the centre of the flour.

2   Add the oil, honey and warm water to the hole. Secure the lid again. Select Variable Speed 10 (or maximum for your machine). Pulse the machine 4 or 5 times (by switching the machine on and off quickly).

3   Open the lid and scrape down the sides. Secure the lid again and repeat the pulsing and scraping (if necessary) a further 4 times, letting the machine rest briefly in between.

4   Preheat the oven to 220°C/Gas 7. Brush two 35cm pizza pans with olive oil. Dust a work surface with cornmeal. Pulse the machine a couple of times to lift the dough off the blades, then tip the dough out of the goblet onto the cornmeal. Use a wet spatula to scrape out any dough stuck to the sides and blades.

5   Knead the dough gently, then cut in half. Roll out each half to a 35cm circle and place in the pizza pans, pressing the dough right out to the edges of the pans. Spread the dough all over with 5 tbsp tomato sauce or passata on each pizza. Scatter a quarter of the torn basil leaves over each and sprinkle with the Parmesan. Scatter torn mozzarella over and add a good grinding of black pepper. Drizzle with a little olive oil.

6   If baking one pizza, for the crispest base, bake on the base of the oven for about 10 minutes or until the base is crisp and brown and the cheese has melted and is just beginning to brown in places (watch it carefully because the bottom of the oven is very hot and the base can burn if you overcook it). If baking two, put one on the lowest shelf and one on the base of the oven and swap halfway through cooking.

7   Remove from the oven, add another drizzle of olive oil and a grinding of black pepper. Scatter the remaining torn basil leaves over and throw on a handful or rocket, if using. Serve straight away.

CHAPTER 10

FROZEN ASSETS

This machine is so clever it doesn't just heat soups and purées, it can freeze them as well. The motor is so powerful that it can blend ice into a mixture so quickly that the mixture remains frozen and ready to serve straight away. The best flavour, I found, was obtained using frozen fruit with just cream and/or custard added (see page 140) but you can also make a whole variety of recipes using fresh ingredients plus a load of ice cubes. Obviously, using that amount of ice gives a milder flavour than ones made in an ice-cream maker but for a quick ice cream or sorbet just when you fancy one, it's great. However, I do find the mixture very soft so I prefer to pop it in the freezer to take out later in the day or store for up to 3 months. Ideally, then, take it out of the freezer 10 minutes before you want to serve it or, if you can't wait that long, dip the scoop in hot water to make it easier to remove from the container. As you need quite a lot of ice cubes, it's worth buying a large 2kg bag of them to keep in your freezer for when the whim to make an ice comes over you, but make sure when you use them that you separate each cube (don't use in clumps) so they grind down very quickly and evenly.

CHOCOLATE HAZELNUT ICE CREAM

Chocolate and hazelnuts are a match made in heaven. However, you can make a plain, chocolate ice cream by simply omitting the nuts. I've not added sugar, just dates to sweeten the ice cream, so this has far more goodness than a normal ice! You can use reduced-fat single cream or even coconut cream instead of the thick double cream if you prefer.

Makes about 1 litre

250ml extra-thick double cream
50g cocoa powder
200g stoned dates, chopped
50g toasted hazelnuts
1 tsp natural vanilla extract or paste
500g ice cubes

1   Put all the ingredients except the ice in the blender goblet in the order listed. Secure the lid.
2   Select Variable Speed 1. Switch on the machine and gradually increase to Variable Speed 10 (or maximum for your machine). Use the tamper to press the ingredients onto the blades, if necessary, and blend for 20 seconds. Add the ice cubes, then secure the lid and blend again on Variable Speed 10 until the sound of the machine changes, about 45 seconds, using the tamper to press the cubes onto the blades. Stop the machine.
3   Serve straight away or turn into a freezer-proof container with a sealable lid and freeze for use later. Remove from the freezer 10 minutes before serving to soften slightly.

COCONUT AND VANILLA SORBET

Clean on the palate, cooling and simple, this sorbet is delicious on its own or served scooped into a shot of rum or pineapple juice, or try it to top a fruit salad or slices of mango. For a richer mixture, you could use a whole 400ml can coconut milk, omit the apple juice and add a little more honey to sweeten to taste.

Makes about 1 litre

250ml extra-thick canned coconut milk
100ml apple juice
2 tsp natural vanilla extract or paste
3 tbsp clear honey
450g ice cubes

1   Put the ingredients in the blender goblet in the order listed. Secure the lid.

2   Select Variable Speed 1. Switch on the machine and gradually increase to Variable Speed 10 (or maximum for your machine). Use the tamper to press the ingredients into the blades. Blend for only 45 seconds until the sound of the machine changes and the mixture is softly frozen. Do not over-blend or it will melt again.

3   Either use immediately or scoop into a freezer-proof container with a sealable lid and store in the freezer. Remove about 10 minutes before serving to soften slightly.

TROPICAL FRUIT ICE CREAM

This is, I think, the best-textured ice cream I've managed to make – and best for flavour as it uses frozen fruit so there's no need to dilute the taste with ice cubes! You can make any flavour you like with different fruits. If the fruits aren't very sweet, you'll need to add honey or sugar to taste, so whiz a bit, taste, adjust the sweetness, if necessary, then finish blending. If you have a glut of summer fruits, freeze some in 450g quantities, ready to make ice cream at will!

Makes a generous 1 litre

400g can creamy custard
5 tbsp extra-thick double cream
450g bag frozen tropical fruits

1   Put the ingredients in the blender goblet in the order listed. Secure the lid.
2   Select Variable Speed 1. Switch on the machine and gradually increase to variable Speed 10 (or maximum for your machine), using the tamper to press the fruit down onto the blades. Blend for about 30 seconds until the sound of the machine changes. Give the ice cream a stir with the tamper to make sure all the ingredients are well blended, then whiz for a couple of seconds more.
3   Serve straight away or scoop into a freezer-proof container with a sealable lid and store in the freezer. Remove about 10 minutes before serving to soften slightly.

YOGHURT, HONEY AND LEMON ICE

This is a light and luscious ice. You can flavour it with vanilla instead of lemon, or even try some stem ginger. Low-fat or full-fat yoghurt work equally well in this recipe but the richer the yoghurt, the richer the finished result.

Makes about 1 litre

250g Greek-style plain yoghurt
6 tbsp clear honey
2 x 5mm thick slices from a large unwaxed lemon
450g ice cubes

1 Put the yoghurt, honey and lemon in the blender goblet. Secure the lid.
2 Select Variable Speed 1. Switch on the machine and gradually increase to Variable Speed 10 (or maximum for your machine). Blend for 20 seconds until smooth.
3 Add the ice. Use the tamper to press the ice down onto the blades. Blend for only 45 seconds until the sound of the machine changes and the mixture is softly frozen. Do not over-blend or it will melt again.
4 Either use immediately or scoop into a freezer-proof container with a sealable lid and store in the freezer. Remove about 10 minutes before serving to soften slightly.

FRESH RASPBERRY ICE CREAM

This is how to make a fruit ice cream using fresh berries or other soft fruit. You can, of course, use stoned peaches, nectarines or apricots or any other berries of your choice. The amount of sweetness needed will depend on the fruit. Use a little honey (or sugar) then, when the fruit is puréed, taste and add more as you need before adding the ice cubes. I find the addition of the splash of lemon juice really brings out the flavour of the fruit.

Makes about 1 litre

200g raspberries
175g clear honey
2 tsp lemon juice
300ml extra-thick double cream
450g ice cubes

1 Put the raspberries in the blender goblet with 1 tbsp of the honey and lemon juice. Secure the lid.

2 Select Variable Speed 1. Gradually increase to Variable Speed 10 (or maximum for your machine). Blend for 20 seconds until smooth.

3 Add the cream, the remaining honey, then the ice cubes.

4 Select Variable Speed 1. Switch on the machine and gradually increase to Variable Speed 10 (or maximum for your machine). Use the tamper to press the ice down onto the blades. Blend for 40 seconds until the sound of the machine changes and the mixture is softly frozen. Give it a stir with the tamper to make sure no more ice remains (if it does, blend a second or two more). Do not over-blend or it will melt again.

5 Serve straight away or scoop into a freezerproof container with a sealable lid. Cover immediately and freeze for several hours to firm. Remove from the freezer 10 minutes before serving to soften slightly.

TOMATO AND BASIL SORBET

This is stunning served in little glass dishes that have been chilled in the freezer, with some baby fresh mozzarella balls, as an exciting starter. If your tomatoes aren't very sweet, 'up' the honey to 1 tbsp.

Serves 4

350g tomatoes, halved
2 tbsp tomato purée
1 small garlic clove, peeled
a few drops of Tabasco
2 tsp clear honey
½ tsp celery salt
½ tsp white balsamic condiment
1 handful of basil
a good grinding of black pepper
500g ice cubes

1   Put all the ingredients except the ice in the blender goblet in the order listed. Secure the lid.

2   Select Variable Speed 1. Switch on the machine and gradually increase to Variable Speed 10 (or maximum for your machine). Blend for 15 seconds.

3   Add the ice cubes. Use the tamper to press the ice into the blades and blend for only 45 seconds until the sound of the machine changes and the mixture is softly frozen. Do not over-blend or it will melt again.

4   Use immediately or scoop into a freezer-proof container with a sealable lid and store in the freezer. Remove from the freezer about 10 minutes before serving to soften slightly.

CHAPTER 11

DELICIOUS DESSERTS

Your high-speed blender can make short work of any lovely smooth, velvety dessert. But it can also make great crunchy bases and toppings, and the perfect wobbly jelly. You can also use it just to whip some cream to serve with another dessert or to fill the éclairs on page 124.

CHOCOLATE AND BRANDY POTS

This uses prunes and a little bit of milk chocolate added to the dark chocolate, rather than sugar, as a sweetener. It's decadent and very rich – smooth and velvety yet firm – a bit like a truffle filling in chocolates. If you are making it for children, you could substitute orange juice for the brandy, but don't serve to babies or toddlers as it contains raw egg.

Serves 6

50g ready-to-eat prunes
2 tbsp brandy
115g dark chocolate, at least 70 per cent cocoa solids, plus a little extra for grating
75g milk chocolate
1 large egg, separated
284ml carton double cream

1 Put the prunes in a bowl and add the brandy. Leave to soak for at least 30 minutes.
2 Break up both lots of chocolate and melt in a bowl over a pan of simmering water.
3 Tip the prunes and brandy into the blender goblet. Secure the lid.

4   Select Variable Speed 1. Switch on the machine and increase to Variable Speed 10 (or maximum for your machine). Blend briefly until chopped and the pieces no longer move. Stop the machine and scrape down the sides.

5   Add the melted chocolate and egg yolk and secure the lid again. Select Variable Speed 1. Switch on the machine and increase to Variable Speed 5 and blend briefly until the mixture clings to the blades in a soft lump. Take out the plug in the lid. With the machine running on Variable Speed 5, pour in the cream in a thin stream. Stop the machine as soon as the last of the cream is added. It will be paler brown underneath with dark, then a splash of white on top. Scoop down the sides and stir briefly. Secure the lid and whiz briefly again until totally blended and evenly whipped brown.

6   Using a hand mixer, whisk the egg white in a bowl until it forms stiff peaks.

7   Add one metal tablespoon of egg whites to the chocolate mixture to loosen it, then gently fold together.

8   Spoon into small pots and decorate each one with some grated chocolate. Chill in the fridge for an hour or two before serving.

RASPBERRY YOGHURT SWIRL

One of the great things about the blender is that the preparation is so easy – you don't even need to core the pear in this recipe.

Serves 4

150g raspberries
2 pears, halved, stalks and calyxes removed
2 tbsp chia seeds
1 tbsp clear honey
250ml Greek-style plain yoghurt

1 Select 4 raspberries for decoration and set aside. Put the remaining raspberries, the pears, chia seeds and honey in the blender goblet. Secure the lid.
2 Select Variable Speed 1. Switch on the machine and gradually increase the speed to Variable Speed 10 (or maximum for your machine). Blend for 1 minute until smooth. Leave to stand for 10 minutes, switching the machine on and off briefly every few minutes to prevent the chia seeds clogging together.
3 Scoop into a bowl. Add the Greek yoghurt and fold through gently to give a marbled effect. Spoon into 4 small dishes or glasses and chill for a few hours before serving.

STRAWBERRY FOOL

Cream whips in an instant in the high-speed blender so take care not to over-work it before you add the fruit. The whole thing takes literally seconds to prepare. Ideally leave it to chill in the fridge for an hour before eating to firm up, but it tastes great straight from the machine. To turn this into a form of Eton Mess, simply scoop the mixture into a bowl when processed and fold in two roughly crushed meringue nests before spooning into glasses.

Serves 4

284ml carton double cream
2 tbsp clear honey
1 tsp natural vanilla extract or paste
1 tsp lemon juice
250g strawberries, hulled

1   Pour the cream, honey, vanilla and lemon juice into the blender goblet. Secure the lid.

2   Select Variable Speed 1. Switch on the machine and gradually increase to Variable Speed 5. Blend for 1–2 seconds. The cream will stiffen almost immediately. Stop the machine.

3   Reserve 1 smaller strawberry and slice into 4 for decoration. Set aside. Add the remaining strawberries to the blender. Secure the lid again. Select Variable Speed 1. Switch on the machine and gradually increase to Variable Speed 3. Blend for 1–2 seconds until pink but still with small pieces of strawberry.

4   Spoon into 4 glasses, top each with a reserved slice of strawberry and chill until ready to serve.

WHITE CHOCOLATE AND LEMON CHEESECAKES

This isn't a set cheesecake, just flavoured soft cheese, cream and white chocolate chilled to firm slightly on top of a buttery crisp base. The exciting twist is the dried mint in the base – it adds a glorious fragrance when combined with the lemon topping. Simple and effective!

Serves 6

For the base
200g digestive biscuits
75g butter, melted
2 tsp dried mint
a little sunflower oil, for brushing

For the topping
100g white chocolate, broken in pieces
6 tbsp zesty good-quality lemon curd
250g white soft cheese
100ml double cream
a little freshly grated lemon zest (optional)
a few tiny sprigs of mint

1 Put the biscuits in the blender goblet and add the melted butter and mint. Secure the lid.
2 Select Variable Speed 1. Switch on the machine and gradually increase to Variable Speed 10 (or maximum for your machine), using the tamper to press the biscuits onto the blades. Blend until the biscuits are crushed and mixed with the butter and mint.

3 Set 6 egg rings or individual flan dishes on a baking sheet and brush with oil. Press the biscuit mixture into the bases.

4 Clean your blender goblet (see page 9). Melt the chocolate in a bowl over a pan of gently simmering water. Put 5 tbsp of the lemon curd, the cheese, then the melted chocolate in the blender goblet and secure the lid. Select Variable Speed 1. Switch on the machine and gradually increase to Variable Speed 4, blending for a few seconds until the mixture is mixed well. Stop and scrape down the sides, then blend very briefly again.

5 With the machine running at Variable Speed 1, slowly add the cream in a thin stream through the bung hole in the lid, gradually increasing to Variable Speed 4. Stop as soon as the last of the cream is added. Give the mixture a gentle final stir.

6 Spoon the lemon cream over the biscuit bases and level the tops. Put half a teaspoon of the remaining lemon curd on top of each cake and gently swirl through to give an attractive marbled effect. Sprinkle with a little fresh lemon zest. Chill for several hours or overnight. You can leave them in the little flan dishes if you've used them, or carefully remove if you've used loose-bottomed flan tins. Carefully transfer the cheesecakes to serving plates. If using egg rings, use a fish slice underneath each one to lift them off the baking sheet, then when on the plates, carefully remove the rings. Decorate each with a tiny sprig of mint and serve.

CHOCOLATE TRUFFLES

Versions of these have been going round for decades but these have a new twist. They're made with dates instead of golden syrup, which give them a gorgeous richness. They're more of a sweetmeat than dessert but you could serve them in little glass dishes, interspersed with tiny boules of chocolate ice cream or arranged on plates with a platter of fresh fruits.

Makes about 28

100g dark chocolate, 70 per cent cocoa solids
50g butter
150ml double cream
3 tbsp rum or brandy
100g stoned dates, chopped
3 tbsp cocoa powder

1   Break up the chocolate and place in a bowl with the butter. Melt over a pan of gently simmering water or briefly in the microwave.

2   Put the cream, rum or brandy and the dates in the blender goblet. Secure the lid.

3 Select Variable Speed 1. Switch on the machine and increase to Variable Speed 3 or 4. Blend for about 30 seconds until thick and smooth.

4 Add the melted chocolate and butter. Secure the lid again. Select Variable Speed 1. Switch on the machine and gradually increase to Variable Speed 2 or 3. Blend until smooth, stopping and scraping down the sides once.

5 Chill for several hours until firm enough to handle (you can do it before with wet hands but it's very messy!). Shape the mixture into 28 small balls. Roll in cocoa powder and place on baking paper. Chill until ready to serve. You can put in tiny petit fours cases, if you like.

FRESH STRAWBERRY JELLY

Don't expect this to be the clear, bright red wobbly stuff of childhood. This is a packed full of fresh fruit and flavour but will still wobble beautifully if you decide to set it in a traditional mould (but for most of us, it's easier just to set it in pretty glasses, which is what I have done here).

Serves 6

2 tbsp water
1 sachet powdered gelatine
450g strawberries
900ml clear apple juice
2 tsp lemon juice
2 tbsp clear honey

1   Put the water in a small bowl, add the gelatine and stir. Stand the bowl in a pan with a little simmering water and stir until the gelatine is completely dissolved. Remove the bowl from the pan.

2   Select 3 of the prettiest strawberries and reserve for decoration. Keep their hulls on but hull the remaining strawberries.

3   Put the apple juice, lemon juice, honey and then the strawberries in the blender goblet. Secure the lid.

4 Select Variable Speed 1. Switch on the machine and gradually increase to Variable Speed 10 (or maximum for your machine). Blend for 20 seconds until completely smooth.

5 Spoon the dissolved gelatine into the strawberry purée. Secure the lid again and select Variable Speed 1. Switch on the machine and increase to Variable Speed 4 or 5. Blend briefly until the gelatine is completely mixed in.

6 Pour into 6 pretty glasses and chill until set. Halve the reserved strawberries (cutting the calyxes in half, too, so each half has half a green top) and use to decorate tops of the jellies.

APRICOT ALMOND CRUNCH

Using dried apricots gives this a wonderful, intense flavour. You could do the same dish with other dried fruits, such as peaches or mango.

Serves 4

160g ready-to-eat dried apricots
300ml pure orange juice
2 tsp powdered gelatine
2 tbsp clear honey

For the topping
30g whole almonds
30g porridge oats
2 tbsp sunflower seeds
2 tbsp clear honey
15g butter
½ tsp ground cinnamon

To finish
4 tbsp plain Greek-style yoghurt or crème fraîche

1 Put the apricots in a bowl and add the orange juice. Microwave on High for 5 minutes. Alternatively place in a saucepan, bring to the boil and boil for 3 minutes, then turn off the heat. Stir in the gelatine until dissolved, then stir in the honey.

2 Tip into the blender goblet. Secure the lid. Select Variable Speed 1. Switch on the machine and gradually increase to Variable Speed 10 (or maximum for your machine). Blend for about 30 seconds until completely smooth. Transfer to 4 large ramekin dishes (they should be about two-thirds full). Chill until set.

3 Meanwhile, put the almonds, oats and sunflower seeds in the blender goblet. Secure the lid. Select Variable Speed 1. Switch on the machine and pulse 3 or 4 times (by switching the machine on and off quickly) until chopped but not too fine.

4 Heat the honey and butter in a small pan. Add the almonds and oats and stir well to combine. Cook over a high heat, stirring, for several minutes until really fragrant and just turning golden brown. Tip onto a sheet of baking paper and leave to cool.

5 When ready to serve, spoon the yoghurt or crème fraîche over the apricot mixture and sprinkle with the toasted almond mix.

CHAPTER 12
SPICE BLENDS AND PASTES

Here's a whole selection of great spice and herb blends to brighten up grilled or griddled meat, fish and vegetables. Making a batch from the various ingredients you may already have in your store cupboard means that, when you fancy a dish that requires a blend, you've got it to hand rather than having to make up a tiny bit, which isn't practical except with a pestle and mortar and that's serious hard work! Keep the 'dry' mixes in sealed containers in a cool dark place and they will last for several months. The 'wet' pastes are best kept, covered in a layer of oil, in sealed containers, in the fridge.

CAJUN SPICE BLEND

A hot, dark spice blend with its roots in South America. Use it to add fire and flavour to chicken, fish, meat or stir-fried vegetables. Rub it on the skin or over the flesh and leave to marinate for a while. Great for barbecuing, grilling or sautéing – I use it in fajitas, too.

Makes 1 medium jar

2 dried hot chillies (I use kashmiri but they're not authentic to the region!)
4 tbsp ground sweet paprika
4 tbsp dried basil
2 tbsp fennel seeds
2 tbsp black onion seeds
2 tbsp cumin seeds
2 tbsp dried onions
1 tbsp black peppercorns
1 tbsp black mustard seeds
1 tbsp garlic granules
1 tbsp caster sugar
2 tsp coarse sea salt

1 Put all the ingredients in the blender goblet or blender container. Secure the lid.
2 Select Variable Speed 1. Switch on the machine and gradually increase to Variable Speed 10 (or maximum for your machine). Blend for 10 seconds, or until the mixture becomes a fine powder.
3 Tip into an airtight jar or other container and use as required.

JERK SEASONING

Originating in the Caribbean, this blend is great mixed with oil and rubbed all over meat, fish, chicken or vegetables before barbecuing. You can, of course, use it for conventional grilling or griddling too. It's worth leaving the food to marinate for at least 30 minutes, preferably longer, so the flavours penetrate deep into the flesh. Although not authentic, I like a hint of lemon in here, so grind in some lemongrass.

Makes 1 medium jar

4 tbsp allspice berries
3 bay leaves
2 dried red chillies
2 tbsp dried thyme
2 tbsp dried onion
1 tbsp black peppercorns
1 tbsp cumin seeds
1 tbsp garlic granules
1 tbsp demerara sugar
1 tbsp sweet paprika
2 tsp ground turmeric
2 stalks dried lemongrass
1 tsp coarse sea salt

1   Put all the ingredients in the blender goblet. Secure the lid.
2   Select Variable Speed 1. Switch on the machine and gradually increase to Variable Speed 10 (or maximum for your machine). Blend for 10 seconds, or until the mixture becomes a fine powder.
3   Tip into an airtight jar or other container and use as required.

MUSHROOM AND HERB BLEND

This is so delicious rubbed on to fish or chicken, in particular. It's also great sprinkled into scrambled eggs or an omelette, and makes a delicious dip worked into some cream cheese.

Makes 1 medium jar

4 tbsp dried mixed mushrooms (about 12g)
1 tbsp dried parsley
1 tbsp dried onions
2 tsp dried thyme
2 tsp garlic granules
¼ tsp coarse sea salt

1 Put all the ingredients in the blender goblet or dry grain container. Secure the lid.
2 Select Variable Speed 1. Switch on the machine and gradually increase to Variable Speed 10 (or maximum for your machine). Blend for 10 seconds, or until the mixture becomes a fine powder.
3 Tip into an airtight container. Use as required.

THAI-STYLE GREEN CURRY PASTE

This is a lovely paste to add to coconut milk to simmer chicken, white fish or vegetables for a simple Thai green curry. I use 3–4 tbsp to a can of coconut milk. I also like to throw in some lightly steamed green beans, cut in short lengths, just before serving the curry. Serve your curry spooned over jasmine rice for a quick and easy meal made in no time.

Makes 1 large jar

6 tbsp sunflower oil, plus extra for storage
2 tbsp lime juice
1 tbsp rice wine vinegar
4 fresh thin green chillies
2 green peppers, halved and seeded
6 green cardamom pods
5cm piece of fresh galangal or fresh root ginger, peeled
6 garlic cloves, peeled
2 tbsp shrimp paste
a large handful of coriander
6 kaffir lime leaves
2 tsp salt flakes

1 Put all the ingredients in the blender goblet. Secure the lid.
2 Select Variable Speed 1. Switch on the machine and gradually increase to Variable Speed 10 (or maximum for your machine). Use the tamper, if necessary, to press down the ingredients on the blades. Blend for 40–50 seconds until smooth, stopping and scraping down the sides as necessary.
3 Spoon into an airtight container. Cover with a thin layer of sunflower oil to keep the air out. Store in the fridge. Use as required.

ALL-PURPOSE INDIAN-STYLE
CURRY SPICE PASTE

This is a medium-hot curry paste that can be used for everything from meat to poultry, fish, vegetables, pulses, paneer or to flavour mayonnaise. It's vibrant with flavour and has a nice bit of heat too. If you prefer a mild curry paste, simply omit one or both of the hot green chillies. There's no need to remove the cardamom husks.

Makes 1 large jar

6 tbsp sunflower oil, plus extra for storage
4 tbsp tomato purée
1 onion, peeled and halved
3 garlic cloves, peeled
5cm piece of fresh root ginger, peeled and halved
2 tbsp coriander seeds
2 tbsp cumin seeds
2 tbsp fenugreek seeds
1 tbsp ground turmeric
12 whole cardamom pods
2 fresh fat red chillies
2 fresh thin green chillies
6 cloves
2 bay leaves
½ tsp coarse sea salt
6 tbsp desiccated coconut

1 Put all the ingredients in the blender goblet. Secure the lid.

2 Select Variable Speed 1. Switch on the machine and gradually increase to Variable Speed 10 (or maximum for your machine). Use the tamper, if necessary, to press down the ingredients on the blades. Blend for 40 seconds until smooth, stopping and scraping down the sides as necessary.

3 Spoon into an airtight jar or other container, cover with a thin film of sunflower oil to keep the air out and store in the fridge. Use as required.

THAI-STYLE RED CURRY PASTE

Another fantastically flavoursome paste to add to coconut milk (3– 4 tbsp to a 400ml can). It's good with chicken, beef, pork or vegetables. I particularly like it in a beef curry with a handful of cashew nuts and wedges of tomato thrown in at the last minute so they heat through but don't lose their texture.

Makes 1 large jar

2 tbsp cumin seeds
6 tbsp sunflower oil, plus extra for storage
2 tbsp lemon juice
1 tbsp rice wine vinegar
5 thin red chillies
5cm piece of fresh root ginger or galangal, peeled
2 red peppers, halved and seeded
5 large garlic cloves, peeled
2 tbsp shrimp paste
2 stalks of fresh lemongrass, cut in short chunks (or use dried, whole)
2 tbsp sweet red paprika

1   For the best flavour, toast the cumin seeds in a small dry frying pan for about 30 seconds until fragrant. Remove from the heat and tip into the blender goblet. Add all the remaining ingredients in the order listed. Secure the lid.

1   Select Variable Speed 1. Switch on the machine and gradually increase to Variable Speed 10 (or maximum for your machine). Use the tamper, if necessary, to press down the ingredients on the blades. Blend for 40–50 seconds until smooth, stopping and scraping down the sides as necessary.

3   Spoon into a clean screw-topped jar. Cover with a thin layer of sunflower oil to keep the air out. Store in the fridge. Use as required.

INDEX